SpringerBriefs in Population Studie

Advisory Editors

Baha Abu-Laban, Edmonton, AB, Canada

Mark Birkin, Leeds, UK

Dudley L. Poston Jr., Department of Sociology, Texas A&M University,
College Station, TX, USA

John Stillwell, Leeds, UK

Hans-Werner Wahl, Deutsches Zentrum für Alternsforschung (DZFA),
Institut für Gerontologie, Universität Heidelberg, Heidelberg, Germany

D. J. H. Deeg, VU University Medical Centre/LASA, Amsterdam, The Netherlands

SpringerBriefs in Population Studies presents concise summaries of cutting-edge research and practical applications across the field of demography and population studies. It publishes compact refereed monographs under the editorial supervision of an international Advisory Board. Volumes are compact, 50 to 125 pages, with a clear focus. The series covers a range of content from professional to academic such as: timely reports of state-of-the art analytical techniques, bridges between new research results, snapshots of hot and/or emerging topics, and in-depth case studies.

The scope of the series spans the entire field of demography and population studies, with a view to significantly advance research. The character of the series is international and multidisciplinary and includes research areas such as: population aging, fertility and family dynamics, demography, migration, population health, household structures, mortality, human geography and environment. Volumes in this series may analyze past, present and/or future trends, as well as their determinants and consequences. Both solicited and unsolicited manuscripts are considered for publication in this series.

SpringerBriefs in Population Studies will be of interest to a wide range of individuals with interests in population studies, including demographers, population geographers, sociologists, economists, political scientists, epidemiologists and health researchers as well as practitioners across the social sciences.

John Bongaarts · Dennis Hodgson

Fertility Transition in the Developing World

John Bongaarts
The Population Council
New York, NY, USA

Dennis Hodgson
Department of Sociology and Anthropology
Fairfield University
Fairfield, CT, USA

The Population Council

ISSN 2211-3215   ISSN 2211-3223   (electronic)
SpringerBriefs in Population Studies
ISBN 978-3-031-11839-5   ISBN 978-3-031-11840-1   (eBook)
https://doi.org/10.1007/978-3-031-11840-1

© The Author(s) 2022. This book is an open access publication.
Open Access This book is licensed under the terms of the Creative Commons Attribution 4.0 International License (http://creativecommons.org/licenses/by/4.0/), which permits use, sharing, adaptation, distribution and reproduction in any medium or format, as long as you give appropriate credit to the original author(s) and the source, provide a link to the Creative Commons license and indicate if changes were made.

The images or other third party material in this book are included in the book's Creative Commons license, unless indicated otherwise in a credit line to the material. If material is not included in the book's Creative Commons license and your intended use is not permitted by statutory regulation or exceeds the permitted use, you will need to obtain permission directly from the copyright holder.

The use of general descriptive names, registered names, trademarks, service marks, etc. in this publication does not imply, even in the absence of a specific statement, that such names are exempt from the relevant protective laws and regulations and therefore free for general use.

The publisher, the authors, and the editors are safe to assume that the advice and information in this book are believed to be true and accurate at the date of publication. Neither the publisher nor the authors or the editors give a warranty, expressed or implied, with respect to the material contained herein or for any errors or omissions that may have been made. The publisher remains neutral with regard to jurisdictional claims in published maps and institutional affiliations.

This Springer imprint is published by the registered company Springer Nature Switzerland AG
The registered company address is: Gewerbestrasse 11, 6330 Cham, Switzerland

To our wives, children and grandchildren

Preface

Since the mid-twentieth century, the developing world has experienced unprecedently rapid and pervasive changes in reproductive behavior. In the 1950s, fertility was high and contraceptive use was very low with women typically bearing six to seven children over a lifetime. Today all developing countries have entered the fertility transition, and fertility has declined to below three births per woman in a majority of countries. The developing world's fertility transition has been one of the most consequential changes of the past 70 years, and a story that all should know.

This book describes these fertility trends, their determinants and consequences, and the debates surrounding them. Many aspects of fertility transition theory and policy have been controversial and the subject of political and academic disputes about what constitutes a problem and how to address it. Our goal in writing this book is to provide an overview of the main issues in these debates and to offer an empirical assessment of the principal research and policy issues.

Today demographers have access to an unprecedented amount of data on reproductive behavior collected through surveys, censuses, vital statistic systems, and other sources. Much of these data are now available online to the international research community. The United Nations Population Division has been in the forefront of collecting these data and presenting consistent online data sets of demographic and family planning indicators for nearly all countries in the world. Throughout this book, we rely on these UN data to summarize the main trends in fertility, contraceptive behavior, and fertility preferences and to illustrate the great diversity among countries and regions in the onset and pace of fertility transitions.

While there is widespread agreement on levels and trends in reproductive indicators, the explanations for these trends and their implications remain much debated. Several controversies and unsettled questions have existed since the 1960s: Which socio-economic determinant is the most important driver of fertility decline? How does socio-economic change affect fertility? Can voluntary family planning programs significantly reduce fertility? What are the costs and benefits of fertility decline? We offer empirical answers to all these questions. We will also place these debates into an historical context, describing both what was going on within the discipline of demography that helped shape these debates, and what was going on in the larger geopolitical context.

Since fertility transitions have consequences for individuals, families, and societies, they are an appropriate subject of public policy. Controversies are inevitable as academics address research questions, and governments and international organizations become heavily involved in policy design and implementation. In the end, we believe that policies should be evidence-based and that it is important to build consensus on the central questions that remain controversial.

This book reviews these debates and summarizes the evolution of policies over the past 70 years. Our goal is to reach a wide audience of students, researchers, and policymakers with an interest in the causes and consequences of fertility trends in the developing world.

Our main acknowledgment is of Peter Donaldson who provided detailed comments on an earlier draft of this book. The support of the Population Council to allow Open Access is also much appreciated.

Saint Johnsbury, USA John Bongaarts
New York, USA jbongaarts@popcouncil.org
June 2022
Dennis Hodgson
hodgson@fairfield.edu

Contents

1	**Fertility Trends in the Developing World, 1950–2020**	1
	1.1 Background	1
	1.2 Fertility Trends	3
	1.3 Analytic Framework for the Determinants of Fertility	6
	1.3.1 Path 1: Conventional Theories	8
	1.3.2 Path 2: Revisionist Theories and Family Planning Programs	9
	1.3.3 Path 3. Coercive Policies	11
	References	12
2	**Country Fertility Transition Patterns**	15
	2.1 Introduction	15
	2.2 Data	17
	2.3 Fertility Trends	18
	2.4 Transition Phases	18
	2.4.1 Pre-transition Fertility	18
	2.4.2 Onset of Transition	19
	2.4.3 Pace of Decline	20
	2.4.4 The End of the Transition	21
	2.4.5 Fertility in 2020	23
	2.4.6 Post-Transitional Fertility	23
	2.5 Stalled Transitions	23
	2.6 Conclusion	25
	Appendix: Country TFRs in 2020 (UN Population Division, 2019)	25
	References	27
3	**Transitions in Individual Reproductive Behavior and Preferences**	29
	3.1 Introduction	29
	3.2 Data	30
	3.3 Contraception and Its Impact on Fertility	30
	3.3.1 Contraceptive Prevalence Trends	30

		3.3.2	Contraceptive Use and Fertility: Cross-Sectional Evidence	31
		3.3.3	Contraceptive Use and Fertility: Longitudinal Evidence	34
	3.4	Abortion and Its Impact in Fertility		38
	3.5	Why Contraceptive Use Rises: The Roles of Demand and Satisfaction		40
	3.6	The Reproductive Consequences of Imperfect Birth Control		43
	Appendix 1			47
	References			48
4	**Socio-Economic Determinants of Fertility**			51
	4.1	Introduction		51
	4.2	Data		52
	4.3	Which Socio-Economic Variable is the Main Driver of Fertility Transitions?		53
	4.4	Education and Fertility Transition Patterns		55
	4.5	Explanations of Anomalies		58
	References			60
5	**Controversies Surrounding Fertility Policies**			63
	5.1	Introduction		63
	5.2	Controversies During the Pre-transition Phase, 1950–1970		64
		5.2.1	From Transition Theory to Advocacy of Family Planning Programs	65
		5.2.2	The Rise of a Population Control Movement	67
		5.2.3	Fears of Famine, Failure and a Population Bomb	69
	5.3	Controversies During the Rapid Decline Phase, 1970–2000		71
		5.3.1	Controversy at the 1974 UN Conference on Population	71
		5.3.2	Questions of Coercion, Reproductive Health and Reproductive Rights	74
		5.3.3	Does Fertility Decline Promote Development? Do Family Planning Programs Promote Fertility Decline?	77
		5.3.4	Africa and the AIDS Crisis	79
	5.4	Conclusion		80
	References			80
6	**Does Fertility Decline Stimulate Development?**			85
	6.1	Introduction		85
	6.2	Age Structure Effects of Declining Fertility		86
	6.3	The Components of Growth in GDP Per Capita		88
	6.4	The First Demographic Dividend		89
	6.5	The Second Demographic Dividend		90
	6.6	Multi-sectoral Benefits from Fertility Decline		92
	6.7	Conclusion		93
	References			94

7	**The Impact of Voluntary Family Planning Programs on Contraceptive Use, Fertility, and Population**		97
	7.1	Introduction	97
	7.2	The Role of Family Planning Programs in Removing Obstacles to the Use of Contraception	98
	7.3	Program Impact on Contraceptive Use	100
		7.3.1 Controlled Experiments	100
		7.3.2 Natural Experiments	101
		7.3.3 Natural Experiments: Adjusted Results	103
		7.3.4 Regressions: Program Impact on Contraceptive Use, Demand, and Satisfaction	104
	7.4	Program Impact on Fertility	108
		7.4.1 Controlled Experiments	108
		7.4.2 Natural Experiments	109
		7.4.3 *Natural Experiments*: *Adjusted Results*	110
		7.4.4 Regressions: Program Impact on Fertility	111
	7.5	Program Impact on Population Trends	113
	7.6	Critics of Family Planning Programs	117
	7.7	Conclusion	119
	References		120
8	**The Developing World's Fertility Transition: 2000–2020**		123
	8.1	Introduction	123
	8.2	Characteristics of the Three Fertility Groups	125
	8.3	Characteristics of Geographic Groups	128
	8.4	The Challenges Facing the Developing World's High Fertility Population	130
	8.5	The Challenges Facing the Developing World's Middle Fertility Population	133
	8.6	The Challenges Facing the Developing World's Low Fertility Population	135
	8.7	Conclusion	138
	References		138
9	**Conclusion**		141
	9.1	Introduction	141
	9.2	What We Know Now that We Didn't Know Back in 1950	141
	9.3	The Benefits of the Fertility Transition	142
	9.4	The Global Consequences of Low Fertility	143
	References		144

Chapter 1
Fertility Trends in the Developing World, 1950–2020

1.1 Background

Fertility rates in the world's "more developed regions" and "less developed regions" stood in sharp contrast at mid-twentieth century. These two regional categories were created by the United Nation's Population Division in recognition of the distinct population patterns, especially with respect to fertility, evident in countries with substantial levels of industrialization and urbanization compared with those countries that were largely non-industrialized and non-urbanized. At mid-century the "more developed regions" already had completed an historic transition from high to low levels of fertility, many having reached replacement levels earlier in the century. The "less developed regions" had yet to see a decline in their fertility levels. In this book we explain what happened to the high fertility level of the "less developed regions" over the past seventy years.

The bifurcation of the world that the UN made was a simple one. The "more developed regions" were Europe, the United States, Canada, Australia, New Zealand, and Japan. The "less developed regions" were Asia excluding Japan, Latin America and the Caribbean, Africa, and Oceania excluding Australia and New Zealand.[1] When presenting aggregate demographic data, the UN has kept this simple "development" division in place even to this day. Of course, as the decades passed the "less developed" label has become inappropriate for an increasing number of countries that started out in the category. We will use the phrases "the developing world" and "the developed world" in lieu of "less developed regions" and "more developed regions" in this work. Preserving these two groupings unchanged over time, while subject to increasing imprecision as much of the "developing world" experienced significant economic growth, is well suited for our purpose. We want to present an

---
[1] Oceania (excluding Australia and New Zealand) never constituted more than 0.2% of the developing world's population during the period 1950 to 2020 and therefore has never affected the developing world's population trends. We will not analyze its population trends.

overview of how 1.72 billion people (68% of the world's 1950 population) with a total fertility rate of 6 births per woman, grew into 6.5 billion people (84% of the world's 2020 population) with a total fertility rate of 2.6 births per woman. The total fertility rate (TFR) is the number of children that each woman would bear if she gave birth in accordance with current age-specific fertility rates. The story of the developing world's fertility transition is a notable one, especially when viewed from its mid-century starting point. At that time no one knew if such a transition would be possible, considering the varied situations of the developing world, and the volatility of its political, economic, and health conditions.

While it is straightforward to paint a general picture of the developed world at mid-century by focusing on the nature of their economies, it is not so easy to do the same for the developing world which had quite diverse economies, polities, societies and cultures. At the time probably the most significant divide had to do with the very different political situations that existed among them. In 1950 half the population of the developing world either lived in colonies with mother countries that controlled their economies and polities or in newly independent former colonies. Notestein had noted (1944: 146–147) that mother countries had colonies "primarily as sources of agricultural and mineral materials, and as markets for manufactured goods," and they failed to foster in their colonies industrialization and urbanization and "that part of their culture out of which the rational control of fertility and the small-family pattern develop." At mid-century decolonization was just starting. From 1945 to 1950 the Dutch East Indies transformed into an independent Indonesia after a four-and-a-half-year struggle with Dutch forces, and in 1947 the British Raj ended on the Indian subcontinent, quickly followed by partition into an independent India and Pakistan. France was still attempting to re-exert control over French Indochina, only giving up that struggle in 1954. African decolonization, sometimes by force and sometimes peacefully, would not end until 1975 when Mozambique and Angola gained independence from Portugal. In the non-colonial developing world internal conflict was also common place. For example, in 1949 the Chinese civil war was ending as the Communist Party forced the Kuomintang off the mainland to Taiwan.

The collapse of the colonial system coincided with a highly consequential sharp postwar drop in mortality. Stolnitz (1955: 53) noted at the time that the factors responsible for the dramatic downturn in the mortality of "the world's impoverished nations" were "all of recent origin" and not the same as those that had lowered mortality in Western industrialized nations: "The primary role of international rather than national health agencies, the use of antibiotics, the development of cheap yet effective methods for combating malaria—each of these is very nearly a mid-century innovation."

The rapid population growth in the developing world that ensued following the mortality decline took on Cold War implications and threatened to thwart the industrialization plans of "Third World" nations, many of them newly independent. Retrograde or stagnant economic conditions were thought to be a breeding ground for communism. For many in the "Free World" this coalescing of historical conditions gave added urgency to limiting rapid population growth, especially in Asia (Taeuber, 1965: 79): "Given the delayed modernization, the synchronization of nationalist awakening and communist political advance, and the coincidence of both these with the scientific and technological advances in mortality control, Asia's problems of population, development, and war become hazards not alone to Asia but to the whole world." Rapid population growth became an important concern for policy makers everywhere.

In Chap. 5 ("Controversies Surrounding Fertility Policies") we will examine a variety of controversies that came to surround policies and programs aimed at lowering fertility in the developing world. Early on the "crisis" atmosphere surrounding rapid population growth motivated specialists and advocates in governments and the private sector in many developed and developing countries to debate the best method of reducing high fertility. This debate took place at bilateral meetings between governments, at a variety of international organizations and NGOs, and at three international United Nations' conferences in 1974, 1984, and 1994. There were also more technical arguments on this topic taking place among demographers. And finally, there was an ongoing controversy surrounding all attempts to influence women's reproductive decisions. Questions of coercion and agency were primary topics at the 1994 UN Population Conference in Cairo when women's organizations challenged "population controllers" on these issues. Knowing the profile that the developing world's fertility transition actually took, will provide insight into the origins of these controversies.

We will trace this transition by using UN data on the total fertility rate (TFR) for the developing world as a whole and for its major regions (United Nations, 2019). These TFR estimates are weighted for the population size of each country. For example, in calculating the 1950 average TFR of the developing world or of Asia, India's average TFR is weighted about ten times more than Pakistan's TFR because its 1950 population (376,325,000) was about ten times larger than Pakistan's population (37,542,000). The resulting fertility levels estimate the number of live births of the average woman living in the developing world and in each of its regions.

1.2 Fertility Trends

Figure 1.1 shows that the developing world's fertility transition passed through three distinct phases from 1950 to 2020. The pre-transition period lasted from 1950 until the end of the 1960s, with high fertility levels remaining near 6 over these years. A rapid decline phase began in the late 1960s and lasted until the end of the century, with the TFR being cut in half from 6.0 in 1965–1970 to 3.0 in 1995–2000. The last phase started around 2000 and continues to this day with the TFR declining only slowly from 2.9 in 2000–2005 to 2.6 in 2015–2020 as increasing numbers of countries reach the end of their transitions.

The pre-transition phase was notable for a number of reasons. It was when widespread concern developed around rapid population growth that was believed to be forestalling the very changes, industrialization and urbanization, that "naturally" induced fertility declines in the then developed world during the nineteenth and

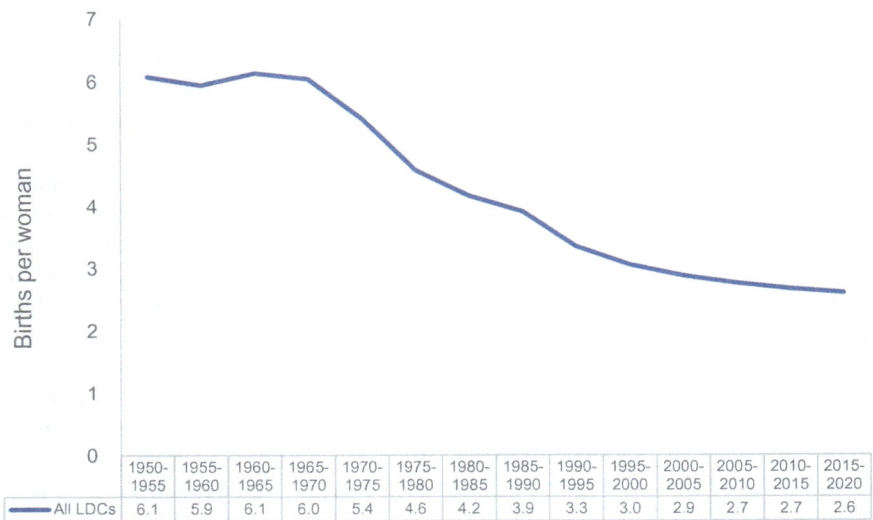

Fig. 1.1 Total fertility rate of the developing world 1950–2020 (UN Population Division, 2019)

early twentieth centuries. Some NGOs and later some governments began launching voluntary family planning programs with the hope of inducing fertility decline in still agrarian societies. These efforts were successful in a number of smaller countries and city states in Asia (Hong Kong, Korea, Singapore, Taiwan) and Latin America (Colombia, Costa Rica, Dominican Republic) during the 1960s, but little happened in the largest countries. As a result, the average TFR of the developing world remained nearly unchanged during these years as shown in Fig. 1.1. Ongoing rapid declines in mortality combined with little or no fertility decline resulted in rapid population growth. Between 1950–1955 and 1965–1970 the average life expectancy of countries in the developing world increased from 42 to 52, their infant mortality fell from 159 to 117, and their under 5 mortality fell from 245 to 177. Absent fertility decline, the developing world's annual rate of population growth went from 2% to 2.5%, and its doubling time fell to 28 years from 34 years. Most economists during this time emphasized the role played by capital accumulation in the development process. The high dependency ratios produced by this rapid population growth increased the need for "demographic investments" for schooling and health care and was seen as limiting the capital available for more directly productive investments (Coale & Hoover, 1958; Enke, 1963). Questions arose over whether there would be enough food, schools, infrastructure, and jobs for the developing world's rapidly expanding populations.

Figure 1.2 shows that the fertility transition did not unfold in a similar fashion throughout the developing world. Both "Asia" and "Latin America and the Caribbean" had rapid declines, and both currently have replacement levels of fertility. They can be considered to have completed their fertility transitions. Figure 1.2 shows that in Latin American and the Caribbean fertility fell earliest, in the late 1960s, and

1.2 Fertility Trends

then declined by about 10% during each decade thereafter. The story of Asia's fertility transition is somewhat more complicated because of the very large role played by China. In 1950 China's 554,419 people made up 42% of the "Asia" population and 32% of the "All" population. China's pre-transition period was normal: a high 1950–1955 TFR of 6.1 and a high 1965–1970 TFR of 6.3. In 1970, however, it introduced its "later, longer, fewer" program: a mandatory later age of marriage, 23 for women and 25 for men; a mandatory birth interval of more than three years; and a limit of two children per couple. Fines and other penalties were used to enforce these rules. During the 1970s China's total fertility rate dropped 38%. In 1979 China adopted its "one-child" policy which further lower its TFR to 1.6 by 1995. The early sharp declines for "Asia" and "All" in Fig. 1.2 are largely due to China's introduction of coercive antinatalist policies beginning in 1970.

In 1950 India, too, contributed a significant percentage to both the Asia (28%) and the "All" (22%) populations. It, too, flirted with coercion during the mid-1970s when Prime Minister Indira Gandhi declared a national emergency and her son Sanjay oversaw a forced sterilization campaign. The program, which was short lived, generated significant opposition and contributed to Indira Gandhi's loss in the 1977 general election. Overall, India experienced a smooth transition with fertility declining between 8 and 11% during each decade from the 1970s through the 2000s, ending with near replacement fertility (2.2) in 2015–2020. It is clear that China and India, which in 1950 together constituted 70% of Asia's population and 54% of the

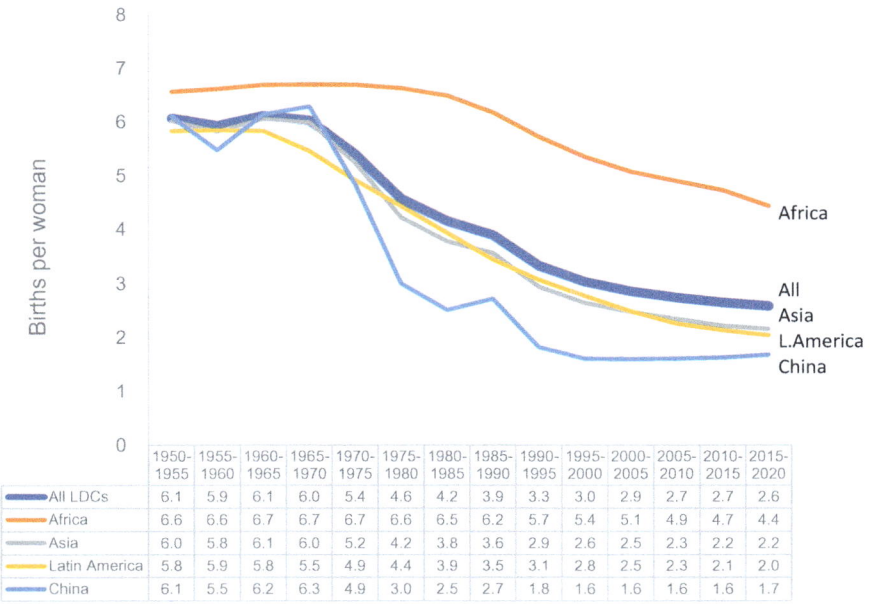

Fig. 1.2 Total fertility rate of the developing world, by region 1950–2020 (UN Population Division, 2019)

"All" population, were largely responsible for the developing world arriving at a low 2.6 TFR by 2015–2020. In fact, the "Asia" fertility trends in Fig. 1.2 are largely a composite of the trends experienced by China and India.

There is more variability among the fertility transitions of the developing world's many other countries. In Chap. 2 ("Country Fertility Transition Patterns") we will focus on that variability and examine the wide range that exists among countries with respect to the onset of their transitions, the pace of decline, and the presence of transition "stalls." Africa illustrates the variability that exists. In Fig. 1.2, it is the obvious outlier. Its pre-transition stage lasted until 1985–1990, and its fertility decline has been modest over the last thirty-five years. Largely as a result of this delay and this modest decline, Africa over time has become a more significant component of the developing world. Its percentage of the developing world's population has increased from 13% in 1950 to 21% in 2020, largely at the expense of China, whose percentage declined from 32 to 22%. UN population projections expect that Africa will have 40% of the world's population by the end of this century. The continent warrants closer examination.

Figure 1.3 makes clear that Africa did not have a uniform fertility transition experience. Northern and Southern Africa appear to have experienced somewhat similar fairly rapid transitions. They both had a clear pre-transition phase that lasted until the late 1960s and then fertility began a noticeable decline. Northern Africa's fertility was at a higher level in its pre-transition phrase, and it experienced a sharper rate of decline than Southern Africa. In 2000–2005 its rapid decline phase suddenly ended followed by a unique slight rebound upward between 2005–2010 and 2010–2015, largely as a result of Egypt's TFR rising from 3.0 to 3.5. Southern Africa experienced a typical decline phase and ended with a TFR of 2.5 in 2015–2020, nearly two children below the average for Africa (4.4). Middle Africa, Western Africa, and Eastern Africa had noticeably different transition experiences. Their pre-transition phase lasted until 1980–1990, with some fertility increases during that phase.[2] By 2015–2020 Middle and Western Africa were still in the early stages of a fertility transition with TFRs remaining above 5. The pace of decline in East Africa has been slightly more rapid, and this region is now in mid-transition.

1.3 Analytic Framework for the Determinants of Fertility

The fertility transition in the developing world was accompanied by many important socio-economic changes. In 1950 18% of its population lived in urban places, and in 2020 that figure was 52% (United Nations, 2018). In 1950–1955 its life expectancy was 42 years and in 2015–2020 it was 73 years. Over this same period its infant mortality rate fell from 159 to 32, and its under 5 mortality rate fell from 245 to 44 (United Nations, 2019). Years of school completed also increased rapidly. In Peru the

---

[2] Middle Africa's increase in fertility from 1950 to 1990 could be due to greater control of STD and a corresponding decline in sterility.

1.3 Analytic Framework for the Determinants of Fertility

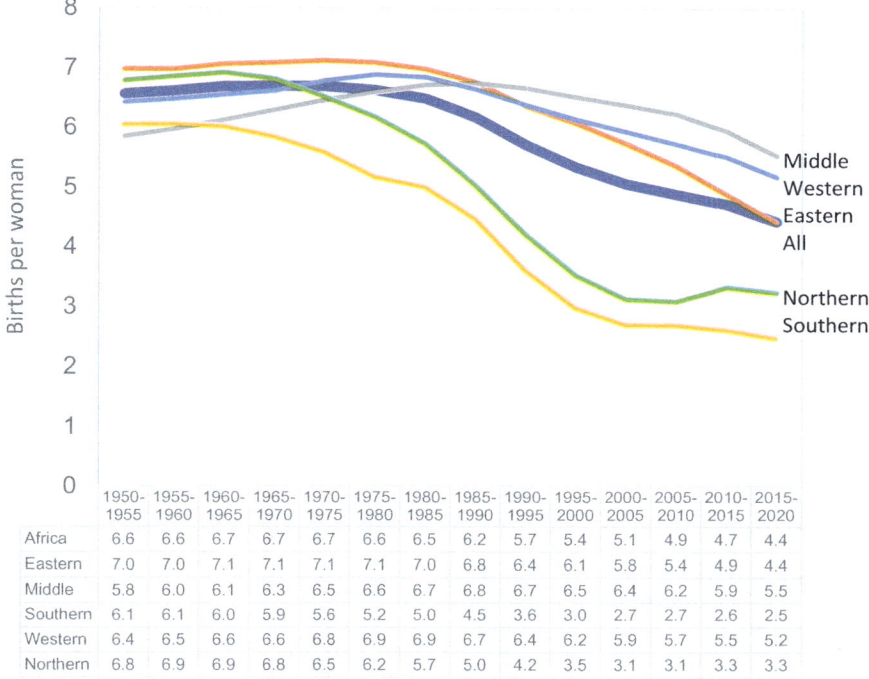

	1950-1955	1955-1960	1960-1965	1965-1970	1970-1975	1975-1980	1980-1985	1985-1990	1990-1995	1995-2000	2000-2005	2005-2010	2010-2015	2015-2020
Africa	6.6	6.6	6.7	6.7	6.7	6.6	6.5	6.2	5.7	5.4	5.1	4.9	4.7	4.4
Eastern	7.0	7.0	7.1	7.1	7.1	7.1	7.0	6.8	6.4	6.1	5.8	5.4	4.9	4.4
Middle	5.8	6.0	6.1	6.3	6.5	6.6	6.7	6.8	6.7	6.5	6.4	6.2	5.9	5.5
Southern	6.1	6.1	6.0	5.9	5.6	5.2	5.0	4.5	3.6	3.0	2.7	2.7	2.6	2.5
Western	6.4	6.5	6.6	6.6	6.8	6.9	6.9	6.7	6.4	6.2	5.9	5.7	5.5	5.2
Northern	6.8	6.9	6.9	6.8	6.5	6.2	5.7	5.0	4.2	3.5	3.1	3.1	3.3	3.3

Fig. 1.3 Total fertility rate of Africa, by region 1950–2020 (UN Population Division, 2019)

percent of the population over age 25 that completed lower secondary education was 18% in 1972; in 2015 it was 62%. In Thailand it was 6% in 1970, and 45% in 2017 (World Bank EdStats, 2021). There have been massive economic changes as well. As recently as 1991 70% of all employment in Bangladesh was in the agriculture sector, in 2019 it had fallen to 38%. Over the same years in China the rate of agricultural employment fell from 60 to 25%; in India from 63 to 43%; and in Egypt from 39 to 21% (International Labour Organization IOSTAT database, 2021). Gross National Income per capita has risen throughout the developing world. In constant 2010 dollars the GNI per capita increased in Sub-Saharan Africa from $340 in 1960 to $1,764 in 2020, and in Latin America and the Caribbean from $4,758 in 1970 to $8,681 in 2020 (World Bank National Accounts Data, 2021).

An important determinate of fertility declines in developing countries was the increasing availability and use of new methods of contraception. They made it much easier for women to control their reproductive lives and greatly facilitated the implementation of family planning programs. In 1950 only barrier methods of contraception existed along with traditional methods such as withdrawal. Over the past seventy years many highly effective methods of contraception have been developed, from birth control pills to long-acting hormonal methods to highly effective IUDs, and many women in the developing world began using them. In Colombia in 1969 only 9% of women used a modern method; 76% used them in 2016. In Indonesia in 1973 only 7% used a modern method; 54% used them in 2018. In Rwanda in 1983 only 1% used a modern method; 48% used them in 2015 (United Nations, 2021). Increases in modern contraceptive use were in part driven by voluntary family planning programs implemented by governments and non-governmental organizations in many countries. These programs provide information and access to contraceptives and reduce financial and social barriers to the acceptance of contraception.

Fertility declines were also facilitated by the growing availability of induced abortion, which became legal for an increasing portion of the developing world's women of reproductive age after the 1970s. By 2017 29% of women in developing countries could obtain an abortion without restriction as to reason, and 22% could obtain one on socio-economic grounds. As of 2010–2014 an estimated 49 million induced abortions, legal and illegal, occurred in developing regions each year, a level that indicates each woman having on average one abortion in her lifetime (Singh et al., 2018: 15, 8).

Why has fertility declined in the developing world? The large number of concurrent changes make offering a definitive answer difficult. We will offer detailed explanations in later chapters. Here we provide a brief introduction to the topic and present an analytic framework for the determinants of fertility that summarizes the multiple factors to be examined in these chapters.

The causes of declines in fertility are the subject of continuing debate. Over time, several theories and their variants have been developed, each with important new insights that are crucial to understanding reproductive change and to the design of policies aimed lowering fertility and slowing population growth. Our framework is summarized in Fig. 1.4. Fertility is determined directly by a set of behaviors such as contraceptive use and abortion. These behaviors are in turn determined by a set of intermediate variables such as desired family size, demand for contraception and the implementation of preferences. The final causal layer consists of the background or underlying variables such as socio-economic change, voluntary family planning programs and coercive anti-natalist policies.

To explain fertility change we propose three causal pathways as presented in Fig. 1.4. The layers of causal determinants are applicable in each of the three causal pathways which represent different drivers of fertility decline.

1.3.1 Path 1: Conventional Theories

Demographic transition theory, first proposed in the 1940s, focused on possible causes of the fertility declines that occurred in the West from the late nineteenth century through the 1930s (Davis, 1945; Notestein, 1945). In traditional rural agricultural societies, high fertility was assumed to be necessary to offset the prevailing high mortality and to ensure population survival. This high fertility was achieved by a near universal absence of conscious contraceptive practices. As societies modernized, economic and social changes such as industrialization, urbanization, increases in

1.3 Analytic Framework for the Determinants of Fertility

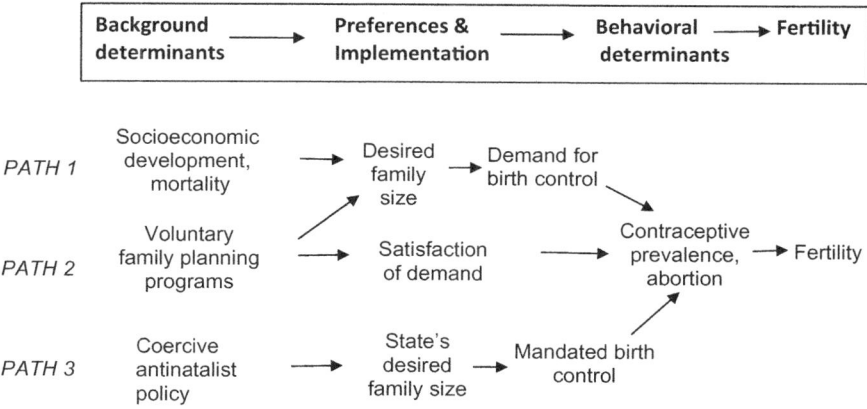

Fig. 1.4 Analytic framework for the determinants of fertility

education, income growth, and declining mortality led to the onset of the fertility transition. The rising costs of children (e.g., for schooling) and their declining economic value (e.g., for labor and old-age security) were the central forces believed to be driving the decline in desired family size. This in turn increased the demand for and adoption of birth control to implement changing reproductive preferences.

This conventional framework, still regarded as broadly valid, has been elaborated by economists, sociologists, and demographers. Contributions by economists to fertility theories have focused on the micro-economics of reproductive decision-making (Becker, 1960, 1965, 1981; Lee & Bulatao, 1983; Schultz, 1976, 2002; Willis, 1974). Parents are assumed to be rational actors who aim to maximize the utility derived from various choices they make, given time and resource constraints. This decision-making includes choices related to conventional goods and services as well as to children. In choosing a family size, parents have preferences not only for the number of children but also for their "quality" (i.e., their education and economic opportunities). As countries develop and incomes rise, parents increasingly want higher-quality children which raises their cost, thus leading parents to want smaller families. This school of thought is usually referred to as "demand theory."

1.3.2 Path 2: Revisionist Theories and Family Planning Programs

Since the 1970s the fertility component of conventional demographic transition theory has been found incomplete in several respects, and questions have been raised about demand theories of fertility. First, a crucial assumption of early demand theories was that the cost of contraception is so low that it can be ignored. This assumption came into question in the late 1960s and early 1970s when evidence documented the frequent use of induced abortion in both developed and developing countries, making it clear that unintended pregnancies were common (Rochat et al., 1980; Tietze, 1981). These findings contributed to an influential revision of the earlier economic theories of fertility by Easterlin (1975, 1978), Easterlin and Crimmins (1985). His framework for the determinants of fertility recognized that the cost of birth control (broadly defined to include economic, health, psychological, and social obstacles) could be substantial, thus leading to significant numbers of unplanned pregnancies. In addition, the new framework acknowledged the role of biology in childbearing outcomes, specifically that without efforts to control conception, women who are sexually active will bear large numbers of children because their reproductive years last decades. Thus, to avoid having "excess" children, parents must practice birth control, a fact that makes the "acquisition" of children fundamentally different from the purchase of durable goods.

A second fundamental challenge to demand theories came in the 1980s when empirical tests of conventional theories using historical and contemporary data failed to find the tight link between development indicators and fertility expected from conventional theories. For example, a massive study of province-level data from European countries for the period 1870–1960 (Coale & Watkins, 1986; Knodel & van de Walle, 1979; Watkins, 1986, 1987) yielded two surprising conclusions: (1) socio-economic conditions were only weakly predictive of fertility declines, and transitions started at widely varying levels of development; and (2) once a region in a country had begun a decline, neighboring regions sharing the same language or culture followed after short delays, even when they were less developed. Likewise, results from numerous fertility surveys of women in developing countries in the 1970s and early 1980s failed to find the expected dominant influence of economic characteristics on fertility (Cleland, 1985; Cleland & Wilson, 1987). Moreover, levels and trends in fertility in the developing world since the 1950s deviated widely from expectations (Bongaarts & Watkins, 1996). For example, Hong Kong and Singapore started their fertility transitions when they had much higher levels of income, literacy, and urbanization than Bangladesh, where fertility decline began when the country was still largely rural and agricultural. Thus, although most traditional societies do have high fertility when compared to modern industrial societies, the fertility transition itself is poorly predicted by customary measures of development.

Another issue left relatively unexplored by early demand theories of fertility is the key role of social norms. Traditional demand theory focused on the reproductive behavior and decision-making of individuals or couples, but largely ignored how this behavior is affected by social norms about how people ought to behave. Such normative structures can be important obstacles to the introduction of new behaviors, such as contraceptive use, in societies where it has been absent. The pattern of social norms also explains why the fertility of women in a given socio-economic class (e.g., highly educated) varies so much between countries. This finding can be explained in part by the fact that the fertility of a woman depends not only on her own education but also on that of her community (Kravdal, 2002): as the level of education within a community increases over time, norms concerning desired family size within that community decline, thus contributing to reduced fertility of all women in the community. Traditional norms, including those that encourage high fertility, tend to become less influential as societies develop and education levels rise.

These unexpected findings required a revision of thinking about the fertility transition and led to the development of theories of the "diffusion" of innovations (e.g., Bongaarts & Watkins, 1996; Casterline, 2001; Cleland, 2001; Cleland & Wilson, 1987; Hornik & McAnany, 2001; Kohler, 2001; Knodel & van de Walle, 1979; Montgomery & Casterline, 1993, 1996; Retherford & Palmore, 1983; Rogers, 1973, 2003; Watkins, 1987). Diffusion refers to the process by which new technologies, ideas, behaviors, and attitudes spread within a population through a variety of mechanisms such as social networks, opinion leaders, and the media. This spread is most rapid within linguistically and culturally homogeneous populations and it is often largely independent of social and economic changes. In particular, the diffusion of information about methods of contraception is now considered an important mechanism of fertility change. New ideas about the costs and benefits of children that may lead to a smaller desired family size are also subject to diffusion processes.

While conventional demographic and economic theories emphasize the demand-driven nature of reproductive change and leave little or no role for family planning programs (Pritchett 1994), the now widely accepted revisionist theories assign crucial roles to the cost of birth control and to diffusion mechanisms. These findings provide a strong rationale for family planning programs that can accelerate fertility transitions by providing information that can alter parents' evaluation of the costs and benefits of children and, more directly, reduce the costs of contraception to those who want to plan or limit childbearing. Family planning programs therefore reduce fertility by assisting couples to satisfy their demand for contraception thus avoiding unplanned births and abortions and reducing fertility (Path 2 in Fig. 1.4). While socio-economic development certainly played a crucial role, it is noteworthy that to date, no fertility decline has been observed in a poor and largely illiterate country in the absence of a strong family planning program. These issues will be examined in greater detail in Chap. 7.

1.3.3 Path 3. Coercive Policies

A third path to lower fertility is for governments to implement coercive birth control policies. China's one-child policy is a prime example of this approach, which set limits on the number of children women can have and mandates birth control to reach this objective. Another notable instance of coercion is India's sterilization program in the 1970s. Coercion of any kind is now universally condemned as an abuse of human rights, and the large majority of governments interested in accelerating the fertility transition have therefore opted to implement voluntary family planning programs. China's experience does have an important lesson to teach us: the three paths to lower fertility in Fig. 1.4 are not necessarily disconnected from one another. In 1970 China definitely started down a coercive antinatalist path to low fertility, but coercion's necessity has diminished over time, as is clear from the fertility response to the recent policy changes. In 2013 China allowed a couple to have an additional child if only one parent was an only child. In 2015 it simply abolished the one child restriction and allowed all couples to have an additional child. As of May 2021, women are now allowed to have three children. Yet there has been no increase in Chinese fertility. China now has over 60% of its population living in urban places, 75% of employment is in non-agriculture sectors, and education is highly prized. Socio-economic development (Path One) is clearly working to keep China's fertility low. Since 1992 over 80% of Chinese women have been using a modern method of contraception, provided for by the government. Universal access to family planning (Path 2) is also a critical factor keeping China's fertility low. Coercion has stopped being the reason for Chinese low fertility.

The main objective of this book is to assess the impact of these three paths to lower fertility in the developing world over the past seven decades.

References

Becker, G. (1960). An economic analysis of fertility. *National Bureau of Economic Research Demographic and economic change in developed countries* (pp. 209–231). Princeton University Press.
Becker, G. (1965). A theory of the allocation of time. *The Economic Journal, 75*(299), 493–517.
Becker G. (1981). *A treatise on the family* (2nd ed., 1991). Harvard University Press.
Bongaarts, J., & Watkins, S. C. (1996). Social interactions and contemporary fertility transitions. *Population and Development Review, 22*(4), 639–682.
Casterline, J. B. (2001). Diffusion processes and fertility transition: Introduction. In J. B. Casterline (Ed.), *Diffusion processes and fertility transition: Selected perspectives. Committee on population, division of behavioral and social sciences and education, national research council* (pp. 1–38). National Academy Press.
Cleland, J. (2001). Potatoes and pills: An overview of innovation-diffusion contributions to explanations of fertility decline. In J. B. Casterline (Ed.), *Diffusion processes and fertility transition: Selected perspectives* (pp. 39–65). National Academy Press.
Cleland, J. (1985). Marital fertility decline in developing countries: Theories and evidence. In J. Cleland & J. Hobcraft (Eds.), *Reproductive change in developing countries* (pp. 223–252). Oxford University Press.
Cleland, J., & Wilson, C. (1987). Demand theories of the fertility decline: An iconoclastic view. *Population Studies, 41*(1), 5–30.
Coale, A. J., & Watkins, S. C. (Eds.). (1986). *The decline of fertility in Europe*. Princeton University Press.
Coale, A. J., & Hoover, E. (1958). *Population growth and economic development in low-income countries*. Princeton University Press.
Davis, K. (1945). The world demographic transition. *The Annals of the American Academy of Political and Social Science, 237*, 1–11.
Easterlin, R. (1975). An economic framework for fertility analysis. *Studies in Family Planning, 6*(3), 54–63.
Easterlin, R. (1978). The economics and sociology of fertility: A synthesis. In C. Tilly (Ed.), *Historical studies of changing fertility* (pp. 57–113). Princeton University Press.
Easterlin, R., & Crimmins, E. (1985). *The fertility revolution: A supply–demand analysis*. University of Chicago Press.

References

Enke, S. (1963). *Economics for development*. Prentice-Hall.

Hornik, R., & McAnany, E. (2001). Mass media and fertility change. In J. B. Casterline (Ed.), *Diffusion processes and fertility transition: Selected perspectives* (pp. 208–239). National Academy Press.

International Labour Organization. (2021). ILOSTAT database. Data Retrieved January 29, 2021.

Knodel, J., & van de Walle, E. (1979). Lessons from the past: Policy implications of historical fertility studies. *Population and Development Review, 5*(2), 217–245.

Kohler, H. (2001). *Fertility and social interactions: An economic perspective*. Oxford University Press.

Kravdal, O. (2002). Education and fertility in sub-Saharan Africa: Individual and community effects. *Demography, 39*(2), 233–250.

Lee, R. D., & Bulatao, R. (1983). The demand for children: A critical essay. In R. Bulatao & R. Lee (Eds.), *Determinants of fertility in developing countries: A summary of knowledge* (pp. 233–287). National Academy Press.

Montgomery, M. R., & Casterline, J. B. (1993). The diffusion of fertility control in Taiwan: Evidence from pooled cross-section time-series models. *Population Studies, 47*(3), 457–479.

Montgomery, M. R., & Casterline, J. B. (1996). Social learning, social influence, and new models of fertility. In J. B., Casterline, R. D. Lee, & K. A. Foote (Eds.), *Fertility in the United States: New patterns, new theories. Population and Development Review, 22*(Suppl.), 151–175.

Notestein, F. (1944). *Problems of policy in relation to areas of heavy population pressure. Demographic studies of selected areas of rapid growth* (pp. 138–158). Milbank Memorial Fund.

Notestein, F. (1945). Population: The long view. In T. Schultz (Ed.), *Food for the world* (pp. 36–57). University of Chicago Press.

Pritchett, L. (1994). Desired fertility and the impact of population policies. *Population and Development Review, 20*(1), 1–55.

Retherford, R., & Palmore, J. (1983). Diffusion processes affecting fertility regulation. In R. Bulatao & R. D. Lee (Eds.), *Determinants of fertility in developing countries* (Vol. 2, pp. 295–339). National Academy Press.

Rochat, R., et al. (1980). Induced abortion and health problems in developing countries. *The Lancet, 2*(8192), 484.

Rogers, E. (1973). *Communication strategies for family planning*. Free Press.

Rogers, E. (2003). *Diffusion of innovations*. Free Press.

Schultz, P. (1976). Determinants of fertility: A microeconomic model of choice. In A. J. Coale (Ed.), *Economic factors in population growth* (pp. 89–120). Halstead Press.

Schultz, P. (2002). Fertility transition: Economic explanations. In N. Smelser & P. Baltes (Eds.), *Pergamon international encyclopedia of the social and behavioral sciences* (pp. 5578–5584). Oxford University Press.

Singh, S., Remez, L., Sedgh, G., Kwok, L., & Onda, T. (2018). *Abortion worldwide 2017: Uneven progress and unequal access*. Guttmacher Institute.

Stolnitz, G. (1955). A century of international mortality trends: I. *Population Studies, 9*(1), 24–55.

Taeuber, I. (1965). Demographic instability: Resolution or retrogression in Asia. In W. E. Moran (Ed.), *Population growth: Threat to peace?* (pp. 60–79). P. J. Kenedy & Sons.

Tietze, C. (1981). *Induced abortion: A world review*. Population Council.

United Nations. (2018). Department of Economic and Social Affairs, Population Division. World urbanization prospects: The 2018 revision, Online Edition.

United Nations. (2019). Department of Economic and Social Affairs, Population Division. World population prospects 2019—Special aggregates, Online Edition. Rev. 1.

United Nations. (2021). Department of Economic and Social Affairs, Population Division. World contraceptive use 2021.

Watkins, S. C. (1986). Conclusions. In A. J. Coale & S. Watkins (Eds.), *The decline of fertility in Europe* (pp. 420–449). Princeton University Press.

Watkins, S. C. (1987). The fertility transition: Europe and the third world compared. *Sociological Forum, 2*(4), 645–673.

Willis, R. (1974). Economic theory of fertility behavior. In T. Schultz (Ed.), *Economics of the family: Marriage, children and human capital* (pp. 25–75). University of Chicago Press.

World Bank EdStats (Education Statistics) portal. Data Retrieved September 21, 2021, from https://datatopics.worldbank.org/education/.

World Bank national accounts data, and OECD National Accounts data files. Data Retrieved September 20, 2021, from https://data.worldbank.org/indicator/NY.GNP.PCAP.KD.

Open Access This chapter is licensed under the terms of the Creative Commons Attribution 4.0 International License (http://creativecommons.org/licenses/by/4.0/), which permits use, sharing, adaptation, distribution and reproduction in any medium or format, as long as you give appropriate credit to the original author(s) and the source, provide a link to the Creative Commons license and indicate if changes were made.

The images or other third party material in this chapter are included in the chapter's Creative Commons license, unless indicated otherwise in a credit line to the material. If material is not included in the chapter's Creative Commons license and your intended use is not permitted by statutory regulation or exceeds the permitted use, you will need to obtain permission directly from the copyright holder.

Chapter 2
Country Fertility Transition Patterns

2.1 Introduction

Unlike Chap. 1 where we described the fertility transition of the entire developing world, throughout this and the following chapters the focus is on the transition experience of individual countries. Policy decisions and program implementation strategies are country-specific. Each country has a special set of economic, political, social and cultural conditions that influence fertility and related policies. A country focus is also necessary to answer some of the most debated questions such as which socio-economic variable is the most important driver of the fertility transition? And what is the fertility impact of family planning programs? (These questions will be taken up in later chapters.)

A quick glance at Fig. 2.1 shows that from the country perspective, there has been a great variety of fertility transition patterns over the past seven decades: many countries have completed their transitions whether fast or slow, the majority have yet to complete their transitions, and a few have hardly begun their transitions. In addition, several countries have experienced a "stall" in their transitions, and it is still unclear whether completion is in their near-term futures. Each country's fertility transition is the result of a different mix of fertility decline drivers (Fig. 1.4), and each hold particular policy lessons.

When summarizing the fertility transition experiences in major world regions, we rely on unweighted averages for various indicators of the fertility transition. Using this measure gives each country's fertility experience equal importance, and allows us to better understand how differing experiences, policies and programs affect the course of fertility declines. With this focus, Niger's fertility decline story is as important as that of India, even though Niger's 2020 population is 24 million while India's is 1.4 billion. In Chap. 1 our focus was on understanding how individuals in the developing world, not countries, experienced the fertility transition. This is why some of the findings in this chapter seem to tell a somewhat different story than those presented in Chap. 1. For example, in Chap. 1 we reported that the developing world's

© The Author(s) 2022
J. Bongaarts and D. Hodgson, *Fertility Transition in the Developing World*,
SpringerBriefs in Population Studies,
https://doi.org/10.1007/978-3-031-11840-1_2

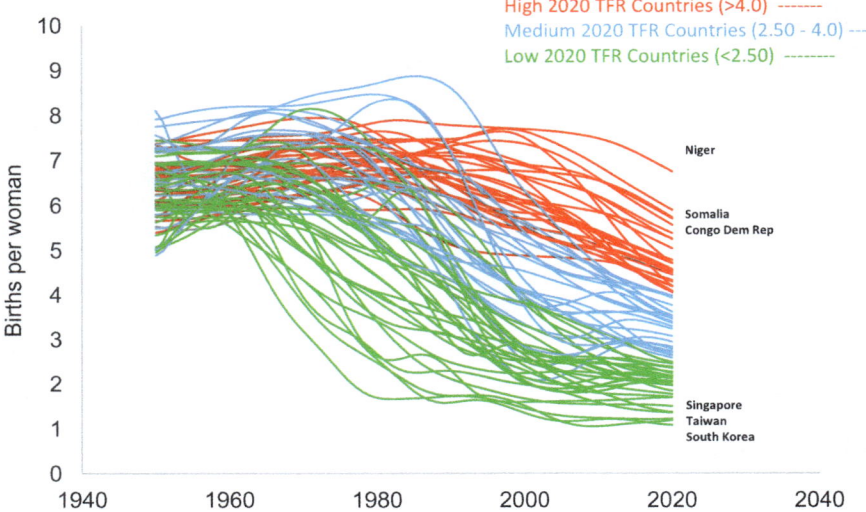

Fig. 2.1 Country fertility trends 1950–2020 (UN Population Division, 2019)

recent TFR was 2.6 (Fig. 1.1), meaning that the average woman in the developing world is having 2.6 live births. In this chapter we report that the average TFR for the developing countries examined is 3.2 in 2020 (Table 2.1), meaning that the average country in the developing world had a TFR of 3.2. The fact that the largest countries in the developing world (e.g., China, India, Indonesia and Brazil) have reached replacement pulls the weighted average below the unweighted average. Each country's fertility transition is an equal source of insight about the drivers of fertility trends, but the number of people being affected by each transition varies greatly. The terms "developing world", "Sub-Saharan Africa" (or "SS Africa"), "Asia/N.Africa" and "Latin America" are used below to refer to "countries in the developing world", "countries in sub-Saharan Africa, "countries in Asia/N.Africa" and "countries in Latin America and Caribbean."[1]

After a summary of the data, the remainder of this chapter consists of three parts: a description of levels and trends in fertility in countries in the developing world between 1950 and 2020; an examination of each of the transition phases, including pre-transitional fertility, the timing of the onset, the pace of fertility decline, the timing of the transition end and post-transitional fertility; and a discussion of countries experiencing a "stall" in their fertility transition.

---

[1] Asia and North Africa are combined in this chapter's country analyses because North African countries' transitions are similar to those of Asian countries, and very different from those in sub-Saharan African countries. In addition, the number of North African countries (5) is too small to constitute a separate region.

2.2 Data

The main source of country level fertility estimates is a databank maintained by the United Nations Population Division (2019). This source provides both 5-year and 1-year estimates of the total fertility rates (TFR) for each country from 1950 to 2020. In Chap. 1 we used the 5-year data. In this chapter we are using the 1-year estimates that are derived by smoothing the 5-year averages. This smoothing sometimes obscures sudden changes in trends and makes the UN data less suitable for the examination of anomalous fertility trends. We therefore rely on TFR estimates from Demographic and Health Surveys (DHS) conducted in many developing countries since the late 1980s to discuss stalls in fertility transitions (ICP, 2021).

Our analysis of fertility transitions in the developing world over the past seventy years focuses on the following 97 countries:

Sub-Saharan Africa: Angola, Benin, Botswana, Burkina Faso, Burundi, Cameroon, Central African Republic, Chad, Congo, Cote d'Ivoire, Congo Democratic Republic, Eritrea, Ethiopia, Ghana, Guinea, Kenya, Lesotho, Liberia, Madagascar, Malawi, Mali, Mauritania, Mozambique, Namibia, Niger, Nigeria, Rwanda, Senegal, Sierra Leone, Somalia, South Africa, South Sudan, Sudan, Togo, Uganda, Tanzania, Zambia, Zimbabwe.

Asia/North Africa: Afghanistan, Algeria, Azerbaijan, Bangladesh, Cambodia, China, Taiwan, Egypt, India, Indonesia, Iran, Iraq, Jordan, Kuwait, Laos, Lebanon, Libya, Malaysia, Mauritius, Mongolia, Morocco, Myanmar, Nepal, Oman, Pakistan, Papua New Guinea, Philippines, Republic of Korea, Saudi Arabia, Singapore, Sri Lanka, Palestine, Syria, Tajikistan, Thailand, Tunisia, Turkey, Turkmenistan, United Arab Emirates, Uzbekistan, Viet-Nam, Yemen.

Latin America: Bolivia, Brazil, Colombia, Costa Rica, Dominican Republic, Ecuador, El Salvador, Guatemala, Haiti, Honduras, Mexico, Nicaragua, Panama, Paraguay, Peru, Trinidad and Tobago, Venezuela.

These 97 countries are selected from the larger set of all developing countries based on the following criteria:

- Population size is above 1 million in 1990. The smallest countries are excluded for several reasons. The quality of demographic statistics tends to be better in larger countries. Smaller countries also often have high migration rates which affect fertility behavior. This criterion means that unweighted regional averages of variables are somewhat more representative of regions.
- Country is pre-transitional in the mid-1950s. This condition is used because we are interested in examining the onsets of transitions. For present purposes a developing country is considered to have entered the transition before the mid-1950s if the total fertility rate in 1955 had dropped below 5.0 births per woman. (The year 1955 is selected rather than 1950 because the early 1950s showed significant fluctuations in fertility, presumably due to the aftermath of World War II).

2.3 Fertility Trends

Figure 2.1 plots UN estimates of the total fertility rates from 1950 to 2020 for the 97 developing countries. Substantial variation in trajectories is evident with Singapore being the first country to enter the transition and Niger the last. The countries have been grouped by the TFR in 2020: High (above 4, red lines), Medium (between 2.5 and 4, blue lines) and Low (below 2.5, green lines). See Appendix Table for 2020 fertility estimates of all countries.

Despite the large country differences there are also common patterns. Fertility is high in the 1950s, as countries continue in their pre-transitional phase which prevailed for most of human history. This phase ends with the onset of the transition, the timing of which varies widely among countries. Once under way, the transition generally continues, and fertility keeps declining. In about two-fifths of countries a new and much lower equilibrium is attained around replacement level before 2020, indicating the arrival in the post-transitional phase. However, in a majority of countries the transition did not end before 2020 and their future fertility trajectories are uncertain. Differences between transition patterns of countries therefore result from variations in the pre-transitional level of fertility, the timing of the onset, the pace of decline, the timing of the transition end and the level of post-transitional fertility.

2.4 Transition Phases

To obtain a better understanding of transition patterns we will examine each element of the transition in more detail.

2.4.1 Pre-transition Fertility

For present purposes we take the highest TFR observed before the transition onset to be the pre-transitional total fertility rate (TFR_p).[2] The second column of Table 2.1 presents the average values of TFR_p for all countries as well as for the countries in each region. The average TFR_p equaled 6.9 births per woman with little variation by region: SS Africa 7.1, Asia/N.Africa 6.8 and Latin America 6.7. However, at the country level TFR_p varies substantially from 8.9 in Yemen to 5.3 in Trinidad and Tobago.

---

[2] The peak TFR is easily calculated in almost all countries because there is only one peak. However, in a few countries pre-transitional fertility fluctuated, and more than one peak may occur before the transition onset. The highest peak is selected unless a secondary peak occurs less than 10% below the earlier peak.

2.4 Transition Phases

Table 2.1 Estimates of unweighted transition indicators by region

	Pre-transition TFR$_p$	Onset year	Onset TFR	Pace of decline (%)	TFR 2020	Post-transition TFR[1]
All countries	6.9	1979	6.6	19	3.2	2.0
SS Africa	7.1	1990	6.7	13	4.4	2.4[2]
Asia/N.Africa	6.8	1974	6.5	24	2.4	1.9
Latin America	6.7	1968	6.3	20	2.2	2.1
Asia/NA + L.America	6.8	1972	6.5	23	2.3	2.0
Africa effect[3]	0.3*	17****	0.3*	−10****	2.1***	

(1) Estimates are based only on the 41 countries that have reached the end of the transition; (2) Only one country, South Africa; (3) The Africa effect equals the difference between estimates for SS.Africa and Asia/NA + L.America

2.4.2 Onset of Transition

The conventional method for estimating the onset of fertility transitions was developed by Coale and Treadway (1986). They identified the onset as the year in which fertility has dropped 10% below its pre-transitional level. This method is still widely used, but Bryant (2007) and Casterline (2001) point out that the year of onset as measured by this approach occurs sometimes several years after fertility has begun declining. To address this issue at least in part, we rely on a revised procedure proposed by Bongaarts (2002), who changed the threshold from 10 to 5%. That is, the onset of the transition is estimated to occur in the year in which the TFR drops 5% below the pre-transitional fertility.[3]

This method yields years of onset for all 97 countries. Figure 2.2 plots the fertility at the onset of the transition (TFR$_o$) by the year of the transition onset (Y$_o$).

The average onset year for all 97 countries is 1979 and the average TFR$_o$ is 6.6 births per woman. Regional estimates are presented in the third and fourth columns of Table 2.1. On average, Latin American countries had the earliest onset year (Y$_o$ = 1968) and lowest fertility at onset (TFR$_o$ = 6.3). Asian/N.African countries are next with Y$_o$ = 1974 and TFR$_o$ = 6.5, and SS African countries had the latest and highest onset with Y$_o$ = 1990 and TFR$_o$ = 6.7.

Transition patterns in Latin America and Asia/N.Africa are quite similar as is evident from the small differences between the values of Y$_o$ and TFR$_o$ in these two regions. This similarity is also observed in Fig. 1.2 in Chap. 1. To assess the difference between SS African countries and the rest of the developing world we estimate the averages for Asian/N.African countries and Latin American countries combined (see next to last row in Table 2.1). The difference between these pooled estimates and the ones for SS African countries will be called the "Africa effect". The Africa effect equals 17 years for the year of onset and 0.3 births per woman for the TFR$_o$.

---

[3] On condition that the fertility decline continues subsequently to reach at least 10% below the peak.

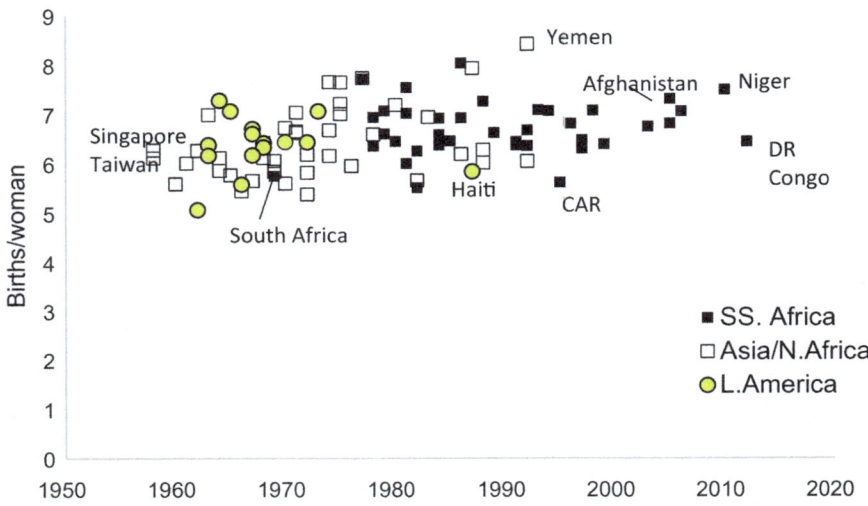

Fig. 2.2 TFR$_o$ by year at transition onset (authors' estimates from UN Population Division, 2019)

In sum, the transition onset in sub-Saharan African counties occurs on average nearly two decades later than in Asian/N.African countries and Latin American countries, and the sub-Saharan fertility level at onset is slightly higher (0.3 births per woman) than it was in other regions.

2.4.3 Pace of Decline

Once a transition has begun, fertility declines continue in most countries. Figure 2.3 presents fertility trends around the year of the onset. The y-axis plots relative fertility (i.e., fertility as a percentage of the pre-transitional maximum level) and the x-axis plots years from the onset of the transition for the 97 countries in our sample. By definition, relative fertility equals 95% in the year of onset for all countries. A decade after the onset, fertility had declined to 76% of the maximum. We measure the pace of fertility decline in each country as the change in relative fertility during the first decade after the onset; it averaged 19% (i.e., from 95% in year 0 to 76% in year 10).

As is evident from Fig. 2.3, there is substantial variation in the pace of decline among countries: in two countries fertility declined by less than 5% in the first ten years of the transition (Central African Republic and Guatemala), while in other populations the pace was more than 40% in the first 10 years (China, Iran, Mauritius and Singapore). Regional differences are also substantial, with the fastest pace in Asian/N.African countries (24%) and Latin American countries (20%) and the slowest pace in SS.African countries (13%) (see Table 2.1).

2.4 Transition Phases

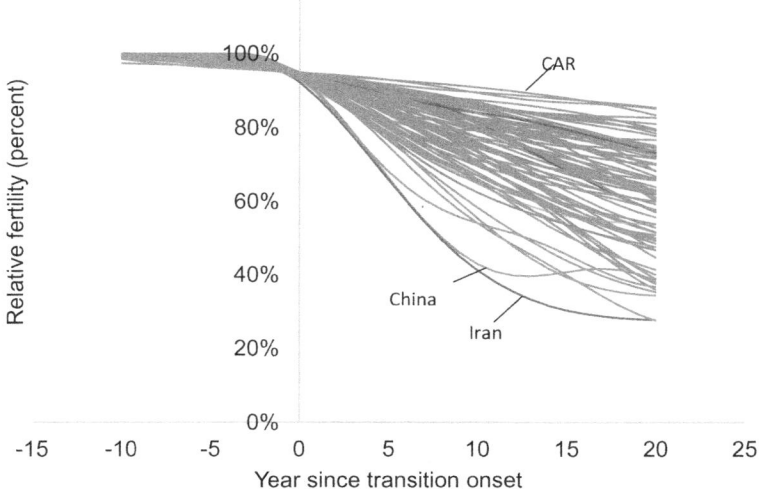

Fig. 2.3 Relative fertility trends around the time of the onset of the transition (authors estimates from UN Population Division, 2019)

A key feature of these transitions is the suddenness with which the fertility levels changed in many countries and the apparent irreversibility of the decline. The onset of a transition usually marks a clear departure from the reproductive behavior of the past.

2.4.4 The End of the Transition

Despite large fertility declines in much of the developing world, the majority of countries (55 out of 97) have not yet reached the end of the transition. We consider a country to have completed the transition if its fertility in 2020 has declined below 2.5 births per woman. By this measure 42 countries had reached the end of their transition.

We estimate the year in which the transition ends for these post-transitional countries as the first year in which the TFR dropped below 2.5. Based on estimates of both the onset and end of transitions, we then calculate the duration of the transition. This in turn allows us to divide the period 1950–2020 into three sub-periods: pretransition, transition and post-transition. Figure 2.4 presents this decomposition for all 42 post-transitional countries. The transition period is depicted in red and countries have been ordered from shortest to longest transition duration. Nine of these countries completed their transitions in 25 years or less, which is very rapid by historical standards: Iran (11), Singapore (16), Thailand (17), Mauritius (18), Korea (20), China (20), Taiwan (22), Viet Nam (23) and Tunisia (25). At the other end of the spectrum are the slowest transitions, with twelve countries that took more than 40 years between onset and end: Philippines (57), Panama (51), Nicaragua (50), Paraguay (49), Dominican Republic (47), Ecuador (47), Venezuela (47), South Africa (46), Morocco (46), Honduras (44), Peru (44), India (42).

This overview of transition durations is limited to countries that ended their transitions before 2020. This is a selected set of countries; the transitions of most countries

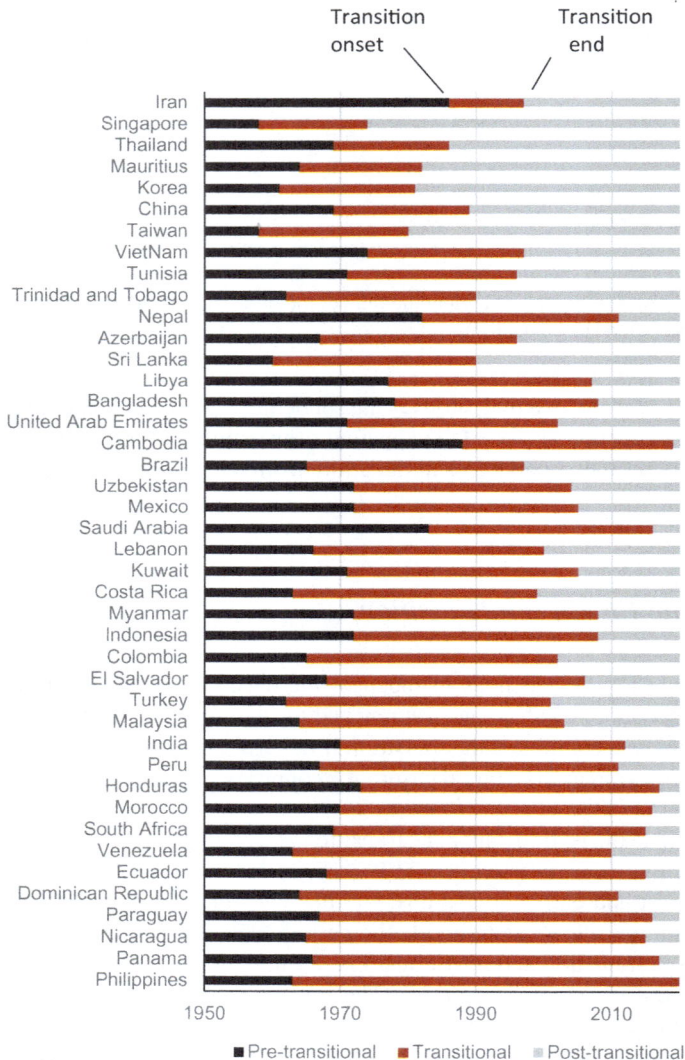

Fig. 2.4 Pre-transition, transitional and post-transition periods for 42 countries with completed transitions (authors' estimates from UN Population Division, 2019)

were unfinished in 2020. As a result, their transition durations cannot be estimated. However, these remaining countries are predominantly in SS Africa, and they have had a slow pace of decline in the first ten years of their transitions as shown earlier. It is therefore likely that most of these countries will have relatively long transition periods.

2.4.5 Fertility in 2020

The record of UN fertility estimates available for this study ends in 2020. All 97 countries had experienced the onset of the transition before 2020 with fertility declining rapidly in many countries. The country average TFR declined by half from 6.9 to 3.2 between the pretransition level and 2020. As shown in Table 2.1, declines over this period were substantially larger in Asian/N.African countries (from 6.8 to 2.4) and Latin American countries (from 6.7 to 2.2) than in SS African countries (from 7.1 to 4.4).

2.4.6 Post-Transitional Fertility

The average post-transitional TFR in 2020 was 2.0 for all 42 countries; 2.4 for 1 country in SS Africa (South Africa); 1.9 for 27 countries in Asia/N.Africa; and 2.1 for 14 countries in Latin America. (All post-transitional TFRs are presented in the "Low" column in a table in the Appendix.) These averages for Asian/N.African countries and Latin American countries are not far from the levels observed in the developed world.

2.5 Stalled Transitions

The preceding summary of fertility trends assumed that transitions generally proceed smoothly over time and more or less follow a predictable pattern. That is, fertility is assumed to be nearly stable before the onset of the transition; the subsequent fertility decline occurs at a fairly steady pace; and the transition eventually ends near replacement level. This standard pattern captures many observed transitions, although, as shown above, levels of pre-transitional fertility, the pace of decline and the level of post-transitional fertility can vary substantially among countries. And for many countries the end of the transition has not been observed.

However, as seen in Fig. 2.1, not all countries follow this standard fertility transition pattern. The most important exceptions from a demographic perspective are several countries where the fertility transition stalled after its onset and before reaching its end. This raises the question of whether some countries may continue to have fertility above replacement for many decades into the future. Stalls can occur at any time after the onset, but stalls shortly after the onset year might be considered fluctuations near pre-transitional fertility and stalls after fertility has dropped below 3 birth per woman may be considered a transition end near replacement. For present purposes, we will focus here on mid-transition stalls which are defined as a leveling-off or reversal in the TFR between 3 and 5 births per woman, a point in the transition when fertility declines usually are most rapid.

In a detailed study of stalls in SS Africa, using data from multiple Demographic and Health Surveys, Schoumaker (2019) identified seven countries in which fertility stopped declining or rose in mid-transition (years refer to start and end of stalls): Cameroon (2004–2011), Congo (2005–2011), Ghana (1998–2003, 2008–2014), Kenya (1998–2003), Namibia (2007–2013), Senegal (2011–2013), Zimbabwe (2005–2011). Fertility trends in these countries are plotted in Fig. 2.5. Note that Ghana experienced two stalls, the first from 1999 to 2003 at a TFR of 4.4 and the second from 2008 to 2014, with a rise of the TFR from 4.0 to 4.2. These estimates are based on the strictest definition of stalling, namely no decline in the TFR. Schoumaker (2019) also examines the record of fertility transitions in which fertility declines between two successive surveys are not statistically significant; this is the case in Ethiopia (2011–2016), Gabon (2000–2012), Lesotho (2009–2014), and Zimbabwe (1999–2005, 2011–2015). The longest stalls are observed in Zimbabwe at 4 births per woman from 1999 to 2015, in Cameroon at 4.8 births per woman from 1998 to 2018 and in Ghana ca. 4.3 from 1998 and 2014.

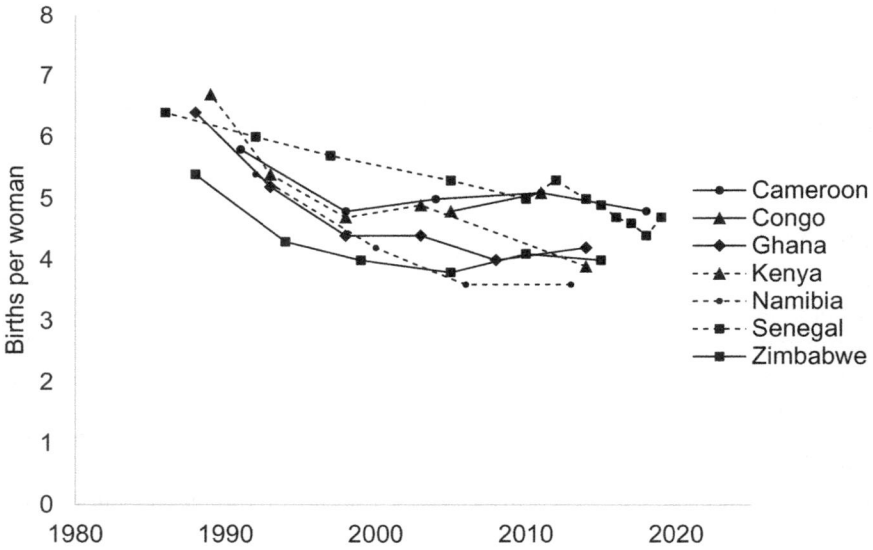

Fig. 2.5 TFR trends in mid transition countries with stalling fertility (ICF, 2021)

A stall is an interesting and unexpected phenomenon, that has been observed mostly in sub-Saharan Africa. But even in this region only seven out of thirty-five countries have experienced a stall before 2020. The dominant pattern of transition remains one with continuous declines.

2.6 Conclusion

This chapter described a variety of transition patterns in developing countries over the past seven decades. Countries such as Singapore, Mauritius, Korea, Taiwan, and China experienced early, rapid and complete transitions. In contrast, transitions in all but one country in sub-Saharan Africa (South Africa) have been late and slow, and fertility is today still well above replacement. An astute reader will note that the first group consists largely of "Asian Tigers" which have experienced very rapid development from the 1960s onward. These countries also benefited from strong government commitment to voluntary family planning programs, with the obvious exception of China's coercive approach. On the other hand, most countries in SS Africa still score low on indicators of socio-economic development, and family planning programs in the region lack government support and remain weak and underfunded. The next few chapters will explore in greater detail the determinants of fertility levels and trends and aim to quantify the roles of development versus programs, that is, the importance of Path 1 relative to Path 2 in Fig. 1.4.

Appendix: Country TFRs in 2020 (UN Population Division, 2019)

High (above 4.0)		Medium (2.5–4.0)		Low (below 2.5)	
Niger	6.74	Madagascar	3.98	Philippines	2.49
Somalia	5.89	Eritrea	3.93	Cambodia	2.45
Congo Dem Rep	5.72	Rwanda	3.93	Panama	2.42
Mali	5.69	Ghana	3.77	Honduras	2.39
Chad	5.55	Yemen	3.61	Paraguay	2.38
Angola	5.37	Iraq	3.54	Ecuador	2.38
Nigeria	5.25	Tajikistan	3.52	Uzbekistan	2.38
Burundi	5.24	Palestine	3.49	South Africa	2.36
Burkina Faso	5.03	Papua N Guinea	3.48	Morocco	2.35
Tanzania	4.77	Zimbabwe	3.46	Nicaragua	2.35
Mozambique	4.71	Pakistan	3.39	Dominican Rep	2.30

(continued)

(continued)

High (above 4.0)		Medium (2.5–4.0)		Low (below 2.5)	
Uganda	4.70	Kenya	3.37	Indonesia	2.27
Benin	4.70	Namibia	3.29	Saudi Arabia	2.24
Cen African Rep	4.57	Egypt	3.24	Venezuela	2.23
Guinea	4.55	Lesotho	3.07	Peru	2.21
South Sudan	4.54	Algeria	2.94	India	2.18
Cote d'Ivoire	4.54	Haiti	2.84	Libya	2.18
Zambia	4.50	Mongolia	2.83	Sri Lanka	2.17
Senegal	4.49	Botswana	2.80	Tunisia	2.15
Mauritania	4.45	Oman	2.78	Iran	2.14
Cameroon	4.44	Guatemala	2.78	Myanmar	2.12
Congo (Braz)	4.32	Syria	2.73	Mexico	2.08
Sudan	4.29	Turkmenistan	2.70	Kuwait	2.07
Togo	4.20	Bolivia	2.65	Lebanon	2.06
Liberia	4.18	Jordan	2.64	Viet Nam	2.05
Afghanistan	4.18	Laos	2.58	Azerbaijan	2.04
Sierra Leone	4.08			Turkey	2.04
Malawi	4.06			El Salvador	2.00
Ethiopia	4.05			Bangladesh	1.99
				Malaysia	1.97
				Nepal	1.85
				Colombia	1.77
				Costa Rica	1.72
				Brazil	1.71
				China	1.70
				Trini & Tobago	1.70
				Thailand	1.50
				U Arab Emirates	1.37
				Mauritius	1.36
				Singapore	1.22
				Taiwan	1.19
				Korea	1.08

References

Bongaarts, J. (2002). The end of the fertility transition in the developing world. In: Completing the fertility transition (pp. 288–307). Department of Economic and Social Affairs, Population Division, ESA/P/WP.172/Rev.1. United Nations.

Bryant, J. (2007). Theories of fertility decline and the evidence from development indicators. *Population and Development Review, 33*(1), 101–127.

Casterline, J. B. (2001). The pace of fertility transition: national patterns in the second half of the twentieth century. *Population and Development Review 27*(Supp.), 17–52.

Coale, A. J., & Treadway, R. (1986). A summary of the changing distribution of overall fertility, marital fertility, and the proportion married in the provinces of Europe. In: A. Coale & S. Watkins S (Eds.), *The decline of fertility in Europe* (pp. 31–181). Princeton University Press.

Schoumaker, B. (2019). Stalls in fertility transitions in sub-Saharan Africa: Revisiting the evidence. *Studies in Family Planning, 50*(3), 257–278.

ICF. (2021). The DHS program STATcompiler. Retrieved September 29, 2021, from http://www.statcompiler.com.

United Nations Population Division. (2019). World population prospects 2019, Online Edition. Rev.1. Department of Economic and Social Affairs, United Nations.

Open Access This chapter is licensed under the terms of the Creative Commons Attribution 4.0 International License (http://creativecommons.org/licenses/by/4.0/), which permits use, sharing, adaptation, distribution and reproduction in any medium or format, as long as you give appropriate credit to the original author(s) and the source, provide a link to the Creative Commons license and indicate if changes were made.

The images or other third party material in this chapter are included in the chapter's Creative Commons license, unless indicated otherwise in a credit line to the material. If material is not included in the chapter's Creative Commons license and your intended use is not permitted by statutory regulation or exceeds the permitted use, you will need to obtain permission directly from the copyright holder.

Chapter 3
Transitions in Individual Reproductive Behavior and Preferences

3.1 Introduction

Chaps. 1 and 2 described fertility transitions from the global and country perspectives. We turn now to an examination of fertility transitions from the perspective of individual women and to the behaviors that bring about declines in fertility. We document what women do to achieve a smaller family size and the extent to which these efforts are successful.

In pre-transitional societies women and couples do little or no planning about childbearing and essentially let nature take its course while observing social norms regarding behaviors that can affect fertility (e.g., age at marriage). This situation changes fundamentally once desired family size declines. To achieve a smaller family size, women must start using contraception (or abortion), a behavior that is new and unfamiliar to most women in pre-transitional societies. As desired fertility declines contraceptive use rises and by the end of the transition women rely on contraception for most of their reproductive lives to achieve a small family size and to avoid unplanned pregnancies. Induced abortion also reduces fertility, but a rise in contraceptive use is the dominant cause of low fertility in most populations.

The first part of this chapter describes levels and trends in contraceptive use and abortion, as well as their impact on fertility. The second part reviews trends in fertility preferences that bring about the rise in contraceptive use. It also discusses the universal finding that some women who don't want to get pregnant are not using contraception. These women are considered to have an "unmet need" for contraception which is caused by a number of obstacles women face in trying to implement their reproductive intentions and results in unplanned pregnancies. The chapter concludes with an examination of levels and trends in unplanned pregnancy rates and their reproductive outcomes over the course of the fertility transition.

© The Author(s) 2022
J. Bongaarts and D. Hodgson, *Fertility Transition in the Developing World*,
SpringerBriefs in Population Studies,
https://doi.org/10.1007/978-3-031-11840-1_3

3.2 Data

- ***Contraception.*** The United Nations Population Division maintains two data banks related to contraceptive behavior. The first compiles estimates of contraceptive prevalence (by method), unmet need, and the demand for contraception from surveys that provide data in a consistent format. These estimates are only available for selected years and come from different sources. As a result, time series of these data are not smooth and there are inconsistencies among sources. To address this issue and to obtain annual estimates the UN also fits models to the observed data. This yields smooth annual estimates of contraceptive prevalence from 1970 to 2015 which we rely on below (United Nations Population Division, 2021)[1]
- ***Abortion.*** Estimates of abortion rates for individual developing countries are difficult to obtain. Because abortion is heavily restricted by law or even prohibited, women are often reluctant to report having had an abortion. Nevertheless, the Guttmacher Institute, using sophisticated estimation techniques, has estimated abortion rates by region for the developing world (Bearack et al., 2020).
- ***Desired family size.*** Demographic and Health Surveys (DHS) routinely ask women about their ideal family size. These estimates are available from the DHS STATcompiler data bank (ICF, 2021).

3.3 Contraception and Its Impact on Fertility

3.3.1 Contraceptive Prevalence Trends

Figure 3.1 plots trends in contraceptive prevalence rates among married/in union women (CPR) from 1970 to 2015 for 97 developing countries. The thick lines represent regional averages.

The CPR rises in all countries between 1970 and 2015. This is as expected from the fertility declines presented earlier in Fig. 2.1. A few countries experience brief periods of decline, typically associated with wars or major disasters, but these pauses are temporary, and the CPR continues its rise afterwards.

In 1970 the average CPR for all countries stood at 16%, with regional averages ranging from a low of 5% in SS.Africa to 21% in Asia/N.Africa and 27% in L. America. Nearly half of all countries—mostly in SS Africa—still had CPR levels in the single digits. At the other extreme two countries—Singapore and Brazil—had CPRs above 60%.

By 2015 contraception was much more prevalent everywhere. The average for all countries more than tripled since 1970, reaching 48% in 2015. The largest increase

---

[1] Since estimates of the prevalence of and the demand for contraception require special surveys which are relatively infrequent, we only use data up to 2015 which are more reliable than those for years between 2015 and 2020.

3.3 Contraception and Its Impact on Fertility

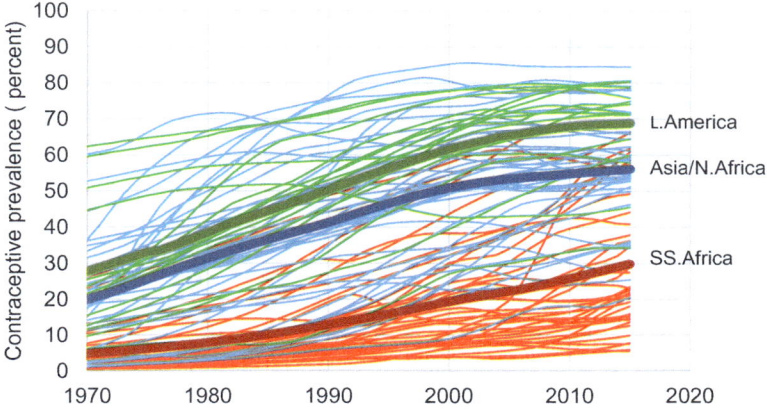

Fig. 3.1 Contraceptive prevalence by country, 1970–2015 (United Nations, 2021)

occurred in Latin America (from 28 to 69%), next is Asia/N.Africa (from 21 to 56%) and the smallest rise is observed in SS Africa (from 5 to 30%).

At the country level CPR increases between 1970 and 2015 varied widely in all regions. At one end of the spectrum are countries such as Chad, Eritrea and Sudan with increases of less than 10% points. In contrast, a third of countries in Asia/N.Africa and L.America experienced surges in CPR of 50% points or more. Such large increases were rarer in SS.Africa, but Botswana, Kenya, Malawi and Rwanda also saw jumps in their CPR in excess of 50% points.

3.3.2 Contraceptive Use and Fertility: Cross-Sectional Evidence

Women (or their husbands) who practice contraception intend to avoid pregnancy. It is therefore not surprising that the contraceptive prevalence rate (CPR) among women in union in a population is negatively and causally related to its level of fertility. This relationship is one of the most widely documented in the population literature. Typically, the total fertility rate (TFR) is around six to seven births per woman in countries with no contraceptive use, while fertility is near two births per woman in countries in which the CPR is about 75% (lower in populations with significant resort to abortion). This inverse relationship has been repeatedly documented using cross-sectional data from large numbers of countries (Bongaarts, 1984; Jain et al., 2014; Mauldin & Segal, 1988; Tsui, 2001; United Nations Population Division, 2000; Westoff & Bankole, 1991).

Figure 3.2 repeats this exercise for the 97 countries in our sample. The regression line fitted to the data turns out as expected on theoretical grounds. Countries with the

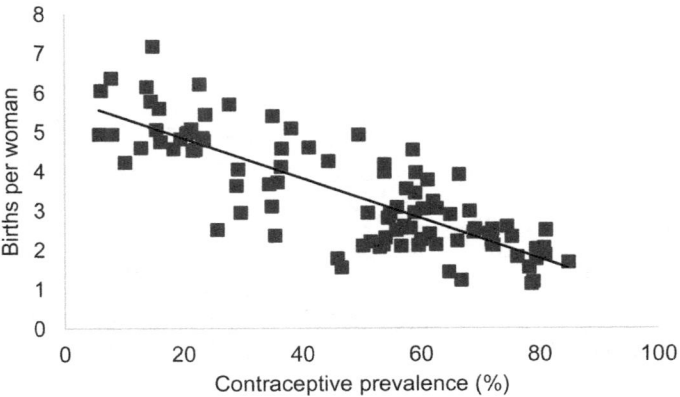

Fig. 3.2 Total fertility rate by contraceptive prevalence in 97 countries, 2015 (United Nations, 2019, 2021)

lowest levels of CPR have the highest fertility levels and countries with the highest CPRs have fertility near 2 births per woman.

Individual countries have CPRs ranging from 6 to 84%, with the corresponding TFRs generally lower the higher the CPR. The slope of the regression line is a simple indicator of the average effect of the CPR on the TFR; it equals a 0.051 births per woman decline in the TFR for each 1% increase in CPR. This is equivalent to a 19.5% increase in the CPR for a decline of 1 birth per woman in the TFR.

As shown in Fig. 3.2, there is a clear and highly significant inverse correlation between countries' TFRs and CPRs. However, many individual countries deviate substantially from the expected level predicted by the regression line, falling either above or below it. For example, countries with a CPR near 50% have TFRs ranging from less than 2 to 5 births per woman. There are several reasons for this finding:

(1) *Variation in pre-transitional fertility.* The nature of pre-transitional fertility has been the subject of numerous studies in historical populations (Coale & Watkins, 1986; Henry, 1961; Knodel & van de Walle, 1979; van de Walle, 1992). A key conclusion from this research is that pre-transitional fertility is largely "natural," that is, the large majority of couples do not consciously practice birth control to limit the number of children they have. This conclusion is confirmed in contemporary fertility surveys, in which couples have been asked directly about their birth control practices. For example, in DHS surveys in pre-transitional societies only a very small percentage of women report practicing contraception (see SS. African countries in 1970 in Fig. 3.1).

The term "natural" is not an ideal one because it can be misinterpreted as being the biological limit to childbearing. This is not the case because natural fertility is affected by non-biological factors (Bongaarts & Potter, 1983). Practices such as prolonged breastfeeding or post-partum abstinence lower fertility well below its biological maximum, yet they are considered natural if they are not deliberately modified as the number of children already born rises. Late marriage and low frequency of intercourse also reduce natural fertility. Natural fertility is highest in populations with low ages at marriage, short durations of breastfeeding, and high frequency of intercourse, and it is lowest when marriage is late, breastfeeding long and frequency of intercourse low. These behaviors are in turn, largely determined by community norms and customs and are thus under social control (Watkins, 1991). As a result, the level of natural fertility varies among societies and over time within a society. As Fig. 2.1 showed, pre-transitional TFR in the 1950s ranged widely from 5.3 in Trinidad and Tobago to 8.9 in Yemen.

The behaviors associated with high or low natural fertility are at least to some extent retained as countries enter the fertility transition. As a result, countries with high or low natural fertility tend to remain above or below the expected level (i.e., the regression line in Fig. 3.1) as contraceptive prevalence rises.

(2) *Contraceptive failure.* Except for sterilization, all contraceptive methods have a risk of failure. This risk is small for long-acting methods such as the IUD and implants but is substantial for the pill and especially for condoms and traditional methods. Average contraceptive effectiveness is less than 100% in all populations, with the actual level depending on the mix of methods used. Failure rates in countries where most women use contraception to space their births are on average higher than failure rates in countries where limiters predominate. Countries with high failure rates, tend to lie above the regression line in Fig. 3.2.

(3) *Overlap between contraception and postpartum infecundability.* Women who wish to delay or avoid pregnancy sometimes start using contraception before the post-partum infecundability[2] period has ended. This means that some of the contraceptive use is not effective, thus leading to a lower-than-expected impact on fertility.

(4) *Abortion.* The higher the level of abortion, the lower the TFR for a given level of CPR.

(5) *Nonmarital fertility.* The conventional contraceptive prevalence rate used here is measured among women in union (married or living together) while the TFR measures all births regardless of whether they occur in or out of union. This approach is becoming increasingly problematic, as nonmarital fertility has risen over time in many populations. This mismatch raises the TFR for a given level of the CPR.

(6) *Migration of spouses.* In many countries spousal migration both internally and internationally is common. This practice lowers the fertility and contraceptive use in both the sending and receiving areas, because spouses are often separated for prolonged periods.

(7) *War, famine, natural disaster.* These events cause massive disruptions of societies with potentially large effects on reproductive behavior. In particular, fertility declines as couples avoid pregnancies.

---

[2] Postpartum infecundability refers to a temporary inability to conceive due to breastfeeding or postpartum abstinence from sexual relations.

Table 3.1 Factors causing deviation from expected TFR for given CPR level

Factors causing positive or negative deviation
Positive deviation
High natural fertility
Nonmarital fertility
Contraception failure
Overlap with postpartum infecundability
Negative deviation
Low natural fertility
Abortion
Spousal separation
War, famine, natural disaster

Table 3.1 summarizes the positive and negative fertility effects of these factors causing the observed TFR of a country to deviate from the regression line in Fig. 3.2. We will not attempt to quantify these effects due to a lack of data. However, in the countries that fall below the regression line the negative factors outweigh the positive ones, and the reverse is the case in countries that fall above the regression line.

Figure 3.2 includes data for all 97 countries. A closer look at the regional relationship between the CPR and the TFR in Fig. 3.3 yields some unexpected results. In particular, the regression line fitted to the countries in SS Africa lies above the regression line for Asia/N.Africa and L.America. The difference is substantial; for example, in a country with a CPR of 50% the expected TFR of SS Africa is 1.4 births per woman higher than in the rest of the developing world. This phenomenon was discovered by Westoff and Bankole (2001). Bongaarts (2017) examined this puzzle and identified several reasons for this difference including nonmarital fertility, substantial overlap between contraceptive use and postpartum infecundablity, and a predominance of contraception for spacing, all of which tend to be higher in SS Africa than elsewhere.

Another puzzle in Fig. 3.3 is that extrapolation of the regression line to CPR = 100% results in an estimated TFR of about 2.5 for SS Africa. This finding is implausible and strongly suggests that these cross-sectional analyses are biased. This conclusion is confirmed by longitudinal analyses in the next section.

3.3.3 Contraceptive Use and Fertility: Longitudinal Evidence

The data presented in Figs. 3.2 and 3.3 are informative and provide a general overview of the association between contraceptive use and fertility. However, such cross-sectional data can provide potentially biased estimates of the true causal effect of the CPR on the TFR because they give information only about differences between

3.3 Contraception and Its Impact on Fertility

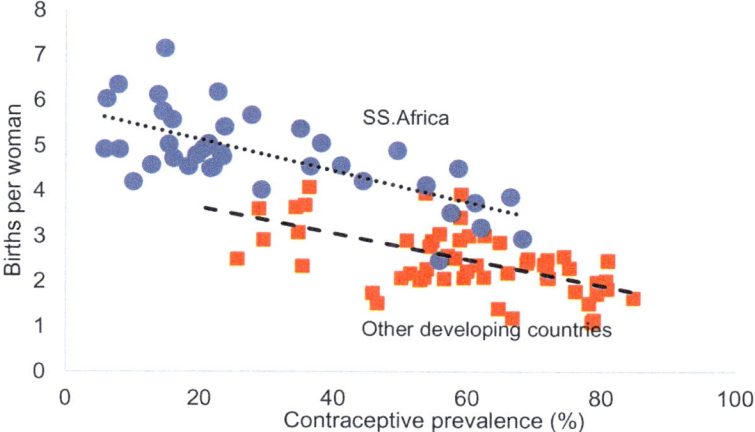

Fig. 3.3 Total fertility rate by contraceptive prevalence in countries in SS. Africa and in other developing countries, 2015 (United Nations, 2019, 2021)

countries at one point in time and not about changes over time. A better approach is to rely on longitudinal data, which we now examine.

Figure 3.4 presents trends over time in the country level TFR as a function of the CPR, thus summarizing the longitudinal association between fertility and contraceptive prevalence. Each line represents one country connecting two observations. The first point on the line represents the pre-transitional stage, with the TFR set at its pre-transitional level and the CPR is assumed to be zero. The second point on the line represents the situation in 2015 with the observed TFR and CPR for that year. (This point is also plotted in Figs. 3.2 and 3.3.) The length of each line indicates the progress the country has made through the transition in term of declines in fertility and increases in contraceptive prevalence, but they are independent of the number of years between the first (pre-transitional) observation and second observation (2015). The lines are shorter for most SS African countries than for countries in the other regions because the former have, on average, made less progress through their fertility transitions than the latter.

As before, the key indicator of the effect of contraceptive use on TFR is the slope of each line which is estimated as the absolute decline in the TFR resulting from a 1% increase in the CPR.

Four findings are notable:

(1) As contraceptive prevalence rises over time, the TFR declines in all countries. The TFR observed for a given CPR varies substantially among countries, but within each region the majority of countries have similar slopes (i.e., the solid lines are parallel to one another). This result indicates that countries start off at substantially differing pretransition levels, but the subsequent declines in TFR with rising CPR are similar.

Fig. 3.4 Trends in total fertility rate by contraceptive prevalence, pre-transition to 2015. *Source* Authors' calculations from (UN Population Division, 2019, 2021)

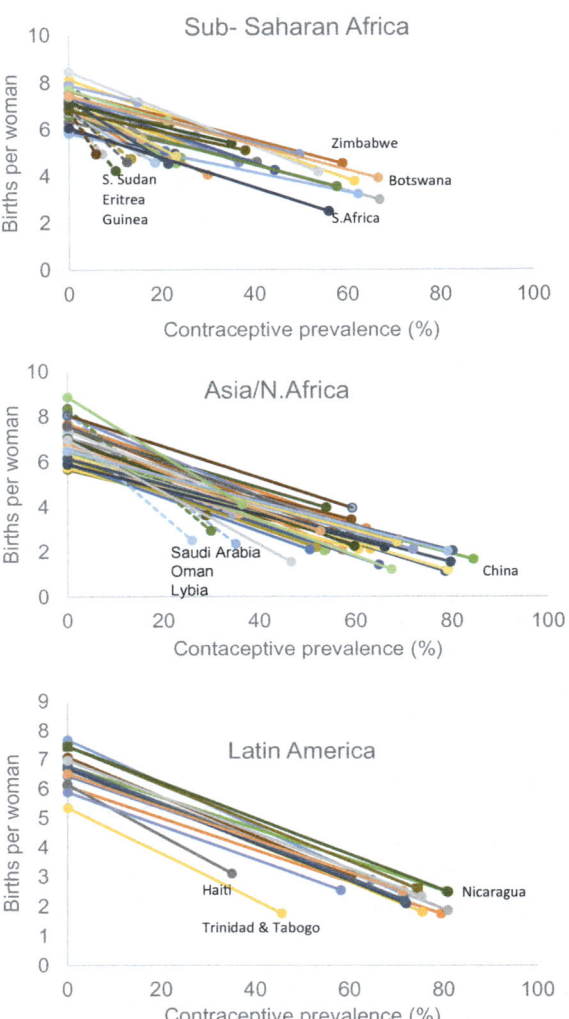

(2) A number of countries have much steeper slopes than is typical for their region (dashed lines). These include Chad, Cote d'Ivoire, Eritrea, Guinea, South Sudan and Sudan in SS Africa, and Libya, Oman and Saudi Arabia in Asia/N.Africa. These countries will be considered outliers.[3] A full discussion of the causes of these anomalous trends is beyond the scope of this chapter, but a few observations are worth making. First, most of these outliers have typical levels of pre-transitional fertility, so the high slopes are due to depressed levels of the

---

[3] Following the standard definition of outlier, a country is considered an outlier if its slope is greater than the third quartile of the slope distribution plus 1.5 times its inter-quartile range.

3.3 Contraception and Its Impact on Fertility

Table 3.2 Regional estimates of the effects of CPR increase on TFR

	Average slope (standard deviation) Births per 1% increase in CPR	Percent CPR increase for one birth decline in the TFR (%)
SS Africa	−0.075 (0.029)	13.4
Asia/N.Africa[a]	−0.076 (0.019)	13.1
Latin America	−0.064 (0.010)	15.6
All	−0.070 (0.027)	14.3

[a]Estimates exclude outliers
Source Authors' calculations

CPR and/or TFR in 2015. For several of these outliers, crises of one sort or another, occurred in the mid-2010s which provide plausible explanations for the deviant slopes in these countries. For example, South Sudan and Libya had civil wars, Chad and Eritrea suffered from droughts, Guinea had a large outbreak of Ebola, Cote d'Ivoire has the highest foreign-born population in West Africa consisting of migrants from neighboring countries. For Saudi Arabia and Oman the depressed TFRs and CPRs are likely due to high proportions of the population (over one third) that are foreign-born migrants, mostly from Asia and Africa, men who work in industries such as construction and women who work in domestic service, health care, restaurants, etc. Most of these temporary workers do not have their families with them. These migrants have low levels of fertility and contraceptive use, thus depressing the corresponding national statistics and causing the countries to be outliers in Fig. 3.4.

(3) Averages of slopes (excluding outliers) differ little by region. As shown in Table 3.2 the average slopes range from a low of −0.064 in L. America to a high of −0.076 in Asia/N.Africa. The average slope for all countries is −0.070. Within each region the country specific slopes cluster tightly around their average as is confirmed by the small standard deviations. The last column in Table 3.2 presents the increase in the CPR required to yield a decline in TFR of 1 birth per woman. For all countries this average increase equals 14.3%.

(4) The slopes derived from the longitudinal analysis are substantially steeper than the corresponding slopes implied by the cross-sectional data discussed in the previous section. For all countries the cross-sectional slope was −0.051 (see Fig. 3.2) and the longitudinal slope equals −0.070. The difference between the cross-sectional and longitudinal slopes (−0.035 versus −0.075) is even larger in sub-Saharan Africa. Clearly the cross-sectional analysis gives a misleading picture of the effect of contraceptive use on fertility.

In sum, an increase in contraceptive use is the key driver of countries' fertility transitions. Over the course of the transition from pre-transitional to replacement fertility, the CPR rises on average from near zero to about 75%. This large increase in the CPR is mainly responsible for the decline in the TFR from 6–7 to 2 births. Other behavioral factors also affect the relationship between fertility and contraceptive use, but these typically have a smaller magnitude. One such factor is abortion which will be discussed next.

3.4 Abortion and Its Impact in Fertility

Abortion (i.e., induced abortion) is practiced at least to some extent in all contemporary societies. The total number of abortions in low- and middle-income countries is estimated to be 69.4 million per year for 2015–2020 (Bearak et al., 2020). Regional estimates summarized in Table 3.3 range from 5.4 million in Latin America to 24.6 million in Eastern and Southeast Asia which includes China.

A widely used indicator of the degree to which women resort to abortion is the number of abortions per 1000 women aged 15–49. As shown in Table 3.3 this measure is lowest in sub-Saharan Africa (33) and Latin America (32) and highest in Western Asia and North Africa (53) and Central and Southern Asia (46).

Interestingly, global abortions rates have changed little over the past quarter century: 40 in 1990–1994 and 39 in 2015–2019. Bearak et al. (2020). This global average could, of course, hide regional and country trends.

Abortion rates are the most widely reported metric in the abortion literature. For our purposes a different indicator called the Total Abortion Rate (TAR) is also useful. It is similar to the TFR but measures abortions rather than births per woman over a reproductive lifetime. In the absence of age specific abortion data, the TAR in a given year can be estimated as 30 times the abortion rate in that year. That is, an average woman is assumed to experience the observed abortion rate in each year during the three decades between ages 15 and 45. Estimates of the TAR by region are provided in the last column of Table 3.3. The TAR ranges from 1.0 in SS.Africa and L.America to 1.6 in W.Asia and N.Africa. These estimates imply that women in the developing world on average have one or more abortion in their lifetime.

Table 3.3 Average abortion and total abortion rate by region

Region[a]	Number of abortions (millions)	Abortion rate (per 1000 women)	Total abortion rate[b]
Sub-Saharan Africa	8.0	33	1.0
Western Asia and Northern Africa	6.7	53	1.6
Central and Southern Asia	23.4	46	1.4
Eastern and Southeast Asia	24.6	43	1.3
Latin America and the Caribbean	5.4	32	1.0

Source Bearak et al. (2020). [a]Regions as defined in source, [b]Calculated by authors

3.4 Abortion and Its Impact in Fertility

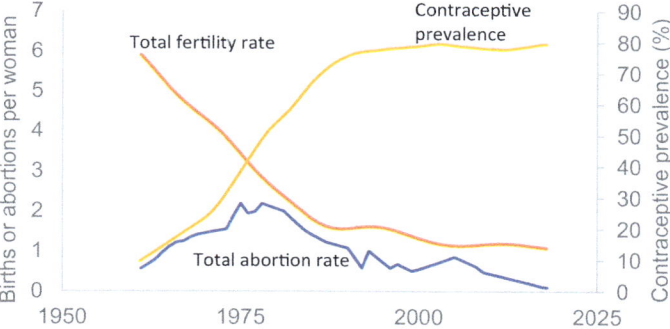

Fig. 3.5 Trends in the TFR, TAR and CPR during the fertility transition in the Republic of Korea (United Nations, 2019, 2020; Johnston, 2021)

These regional estimates provide little insight into levels and trends in abortion rates in individual countries. Reliable country data on abortion are rare, but Korea has one of the best records available in the developing world. As shown in Fig. 3.5, Korea has estimates of the total abortion rate (number abortions over a woman's reproductive years) from 1961 onward, covering nearly all of the fertility transition to replacement. The TFR declined from 6.1 in 1960 to 1.6 in 1990. During this period the CPR rose steadily, leveling off after 1990 at between 75 and 80%. The total abortion rate rose from low levels in the 1950s to 2.2 abortions per woman in the late 1970s. The sharp rise in both the CPR and the TAR reflects the rapidly rising demand for birth control during this period. After 1980 abortion rates dropped, presumably because women became more reliant on contraception to implement their reproductive preferences and the government's family planning program continued to provide ready access to contraceptive options.

Unfortunately, the available evidence is too limited to confirm whether abortion rates in other countries follow Korea's inverted U-shaped pattern over the course of the transition. It would not be surprising if this were the case. One relevant finding from Bearack et al. (2020) concerns the pattern of abortion rates of countries classified by development status. The average abortion rate is 38 in low-income countries, rising to 44 in middle income countries and dropping to just 15 in high income countries, indicating an inverted U-shaped pattern in this cross-section by development status.

Women resort to abortions to end unwanted pregnancies but estimating the fertility impact of these abortions is not straightforward. Past research has shown that an abortion averts less than one birth. There are a number of reasons for this perhaps unexpected fact (e.g., an induced abortion might have been unnecessary if the pregnancy would have ended in a spontaneous abortion or still birth.) For more details see Bongaarts and Potter (1983). Given the estimated TARs a typical value for births averted per abortion is 0.4 in SS. Africa and 0.5 for the rest of the developing world. The reduction in fertility resulting from abortions (estimated as the product of births averted per abortion and the total abortion rate) ranges from 0.4 in SS. Africa to 0.8 in W.Asia and N.Africa.

Levels of abortion are substantial throughout the developing world, but in most regions the reduction in the TFR achieved by abortion averages substantially less than one birth per woman. This effect is much smaller than the TFR decline due to contraception. In general abortion is therefore a less important driver of the fertility transition than contraception.

3.5 Why Contraceptive Use Rises: The Roles of Demand and Satisfaction

As the fertility transition proceeds and desired family size declines women face two key decisions. The first is how many births to have. If desired family size is less than natural fertility, then women will only need a fraction of their reproductive lives for bearing wanted children and will need to use birth control to avoid unplanned pregnancies during the remainder of their reproductive lives. Women who have reached their desired family size ("limiters") as well as women who want to delay the next wanted pregnancy ("spacers") are assumed to have a "demand" for contraception. This demand rises over time as the desired family size declines during the transition.

The second decision women face is whether to use contraception when they don't want to get pregnant. In an ideal world all women who have a demand for contraception would be practicing contraception, but in reality, this is not the case. That is, despite wanting to avoid pregnancy some women currently in relationships are not taking action to protect themselves from the risk of pregnancy. These women are considered to have an *unmet need* for contraception.

The reasons for the nonuse of contraception among women who are motivated not to become pregnant are varied and include: a lack of knowledge about and access to contraceptives and related services, the cost of contraception, fear of side effects, infrequent sexual activity, personal opposition or opposition from spouses and other family members, and from religious or political leaders (Bongaarts & Bruce, 1995; Casterline & Sinding, 2000; Casterline et al., 1997, 2001; Cleland et al., 2006; El-Zanaty et al., 1999). These obstacles tend to be larger in the early years of the transition when women need time to learn how to reliably acquire and use contraceptives and when they may lack accurate information about modern contraceptives and their sources. Having just begun the practice, they also might have less concern about the consequences of an unwanted pregnancy, and therefore might be less vigilant about birth control practices. Offsetting these obstacles are the opportunity costs of having an unplanned pregnancy which motivates women to use effective contraception. These costs tend to rise over time as women become more educated and desire to join the labor market.

From an analytic point of view demand and its satisfaction can be considered separate factors. But from the point of view of an individual woman these factors are linked. That is, a rising demand requires a rising level of satisfaction if women are to accomplish their goal of having a small family and avoiding an increasing number

3.5 Why Contraceptive Use Rises … 41

of unplanned pregnancies during their 30+ reproductive years. An increase in the satisfaction of demand over the course of the transition is essential for achieving a small family size.

An analysis of these processes at the population level requires the introduction of two new indictors:

- *Demand for contraception* (D) refers to the proportion of women in union who do not want to get pregnant. This indicator estimates the level of contraceptive use that would be observed if all women fully implemented their fertility preferences by using effective birth control.
- *Proportion of demand satisfied* (DS). This indicator equals the ratio of use to demand, i.e., DS = CPR/D. As noted, the CPR falls short of the level demanded (D) in all contemporary societies and observed values of DS are therefore less than 1.0. DS is a measure of the degree to which women are able to avoid unplanned pregnancies and, by implication, a measure of the obstacles to contraceptive use.

Figure 3.6 presents trends in the demand for contraception (D) and the proportion implemented (DS) among married women of reproductive age (MWRA) for each of the three regions from 1970 to 2015. (These regional estimates are the unweighted averages of the country estimates). Also plotted is the observed CPR which equals the product of D and DS: CPR = DxDS (when CPR, D and DS are expressed as proportions). In all three regions these indicators of reproductive behavior rose between 1970 and 2015, but, as expected, their values are lower in SS.Africa than in Asia and Latin America. For example, in 2015 demand reached 71% in Asia/N.Africa and 81% in L.America, while in SS Africa demand, although rising, only was 54%. Similarly, the percent satisfied stood at 80% in Asia and 84% in L.America compared to 56% in SS Africa. Throughout the period 1970–2015 the regional differences in D and DS are directly responsible for the still large differences in the CPR.

At any point in time the relative levels of D and DS indicate which of these factors is the most important direct determinant of CPR. As can be seen in Fig. 3.6 in Asia/N. Africa and L.America values of D and DS closely track each other throughout the period 1970–2015. However, before 2000 the DS in SS.Africa is substantially lower then D, indicating that DS was largely responsible for the very low CPR level before 2000.

It may seem surprising that the demand for contraception was as high as 34% in 1970 in SS. Africa when most of the continent was still pre-transitional and desired family size was high. One reason for this finding is that several early transition countries (e.g., South Africa, Kenya, and Zimbabwe) were already experiencing increases in demand. In the true pre-transitional countries (such as Chad, Mali and Niger) demand was around 25%. This may still seem rather high, but it should be emphasized that nearly all this demand was for spacing of births. Given the high desired family size the proportion of women wanting to stop childbearing was typically less than 5%.

Observed CPR increases are driven by rising levels of D and DS. The more rapid rise in DS than in D evident in Fig. 3.6 in all three regions suggests that the former is more important as a determinant of trends in CPR than the latter. To confirm

Fig. 3.6 Trends in unweighted average demand, demand satisfaction and contraceptive prevalence 1970–2015, by region (United Nations, 2021)

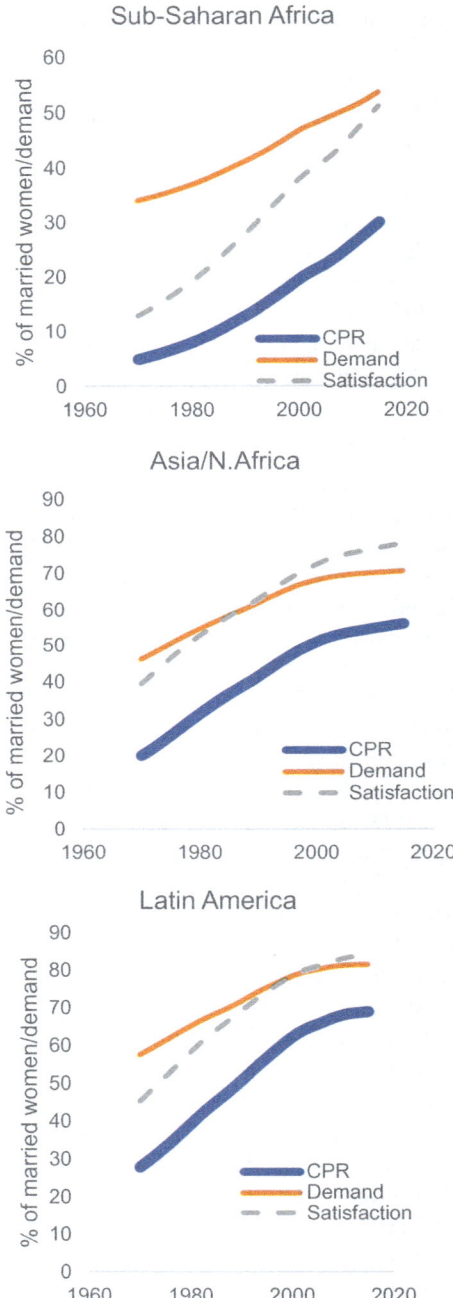

Fig. 3.7 Rise in CPR 1970–2015 and its demand and satisfaction components

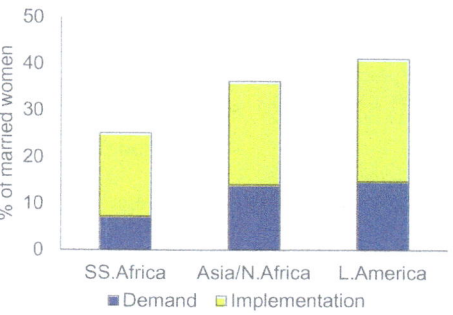

this finding, we undertake a simple decomposition exercise which divides the total increase in CPR between 1970 and 2015 into two components, one measuring the impact of the change in demand, and the other the change in satisfaction. (Details of the decomposition procedure are provided in Appendix 1.)

Figure 3.7 presents the results of the decompositions for each region in the developing world. The overall size of the bars in the figure equals the size of the rise in the CPR between 1970 and 2015. This overall increase is divided into a component attributable to the rise in demand (the blue part) and a component attributable to the rise in satisfaction (the yellow part). These estimates show that the increases in satisfaction are more important than the increases in demand in accounting for the rises in CPR. The average proportion of the change in CPR accounted for by rising satisfaction ranges from 69% in SS Africa to 62% in Asia/N.Africa and 61% in L.America. These decomposition estimates of the dominant role of demand satisfaction are broadly consistent with those of Ibitoye et al. (2022) and Feyisetan et al. (2000) although our estimates are somewhat smaller than theirs.

These findings provide clear evidence for the importance of demand satisfaction as the primary driver of increases in contraceptive prevalence over the course of the fertility transition.

3.6 The Reproductive Consequences of Imperfect Birth Control

In all countries there are some women who do not want to get pregnant and are not using contraception. In addition, contraceptive failures occur among women who practice non-permanent methods of contraception. The inevitable result is that at least some of these women have unplanned pregnancies. This is true even in more recent decades when new contraceptive technologies have become available, and the choice of methods and their effectiveness have risen (United Nations Population Division, 2021). World-wide, 121 million unintended pregnancies occur each year

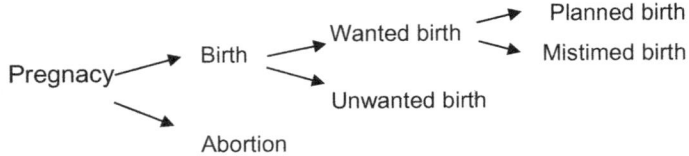

Fig. 3.8 Multiple pregnancy outcomes

of which more than half (73.3 million) end in abortions (Bearak et al., 2020). Clearly contraception is far from perfect.

We will now examine levels and trends of unplanned pregnancies rates and their reproductive outcomes over the course of the fertility transition in the developing world. Figure 3.8 summarizes the various pregnancy outcomes of interest. (For simplicity, spontaneous abortions are ignored.) Any pregnancy therefore ends either in a birth or in an abortion. Births can be further divided into wanted and unwanted types (depending on whether they occur before or after the woman has reached her desired family size). Wanted births can be planned or mistimed (depending on whether the timing of the wanted birth was in accordance with plans).

To quantify the population-level incidence of these different outcomes, we calculate various "total" rates. These rates measure the average number of pregnancy outcomes women would experience over a lifetime if they experienced the current age-specific rates of their population. The most familiar and widely used of such rates is the total fertility rate (TFR) which measures the lifetime number of births given current age-specific fertility rates. Other total event rates presented here are the total pregnancy rate (TPR) and the total abortion rate (TAR). The total pregnancy rate equals the sum of the total abortion rate and the total fertility rate: TPR = TAR + TFR.

The data for this exercise are taken from Bongaarts and Casterline (2018) who estimated the various non-abortion outcomes from the latest available DHS survey conducted after 2000 in 53 developing countries. Abortion rates are based on regional and sub-regional estimates from Sedgh et al. (2016).

Figure 3.9 plots average country-level rates of the various outcomes observed at the time of the most recent DHS survey as a function desired family size (DFS). The DFS is used as a proxy for stage of fertility transition. The horizontal axis is reversed so that early transition countries with high desired family size are on the left and late transition countries with low desired family size are on the right, to correspond to a transition that moves from left to right with time. Countries are grouped by level of desired family size (i.e., 7+, 7–6, 6–5, 5–4, 4–3, 3–2). For simplicity the countries in the group with desired family size of 7 and above will be called pre-transitional and the countries with a desired family size below 3 will be considered to have reached the end of the transition.

The overall size of each bar equals the total pregnancy rate which declines from 7.6 pregnancies per woman in pre-transitional countries to 3.8 pregnancies per woman in countries at the end of the transition. The corresponding change in the TFR is from

3.6 The Reproductive Consequences of Imperfect Birth Control

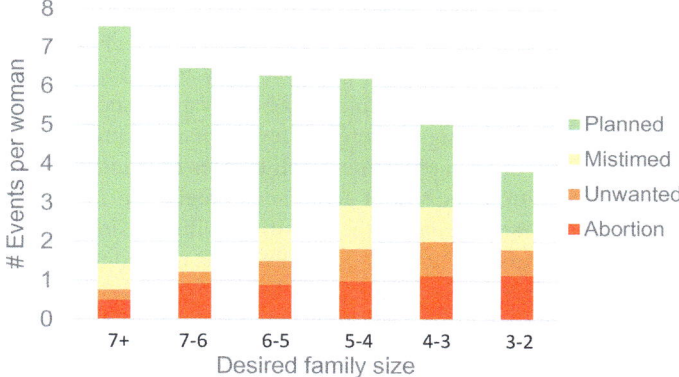

Fig. 3.9 Total pregnancy rate components (planned, mistimed, unwanted and abortion, by level of desired family size, at the time of the most recent DHS survey (Bongaarts & Casterline, 2018)

7.0 to 2.7 births per woman. As noted earlier, the unweighted country average TFR for the developing world equals 3.3 births per woman and the average women's TFR equals 2.6. As a result, most women in the developing world live today in situations represented by the two columns on the right in Fig. 3.9.

The main driver of the downward trends in the TPR and TFR is a large decline in planned births (green bars) from 6.1 to 1.6 per woman with an approximately linear transition from high to low fertility. The trends in the other pregnancy outcomes (mistimed in yellow, unwanted in orange and abortion in red) are not linear. All these unintended outcomes *rise* in the first half of the transition, peaking in mid transition and then decline by the end of the transition, except for the abortion rate which rises and then remains flat. In the pre-transitional group a relatively small proportion of pregnancies (19%) is unplanned and only 10% is unwanted. (Note that this finding is consistent with an average unmet need of 19% in this group of countries).[4] In contrast, at the end of the transition, more than half of all pregnancies (59%) are unplanned. In this group of countries women average 2.3 unplanned pregnancies over their lifetimes, which equals the sum of 1.1 abortions, 0.6 unwanted births, and 0.5 mistimed births.

The main findings from the preceding analysis are that unplanned pregnancy rates are substantial in all countries but are typically highest in mid-transition countries. Furthermore, the *fraction* of all pregnancies that is unplanned is highest in the developing countries with the lowest desired family size. In these societies at the end of the transition almost one-third (1.2/3.8) of pregnancies yield an unwanted or mistimed birth, the unplanned *pregnancy rate* exceeds two per woman, and the unplanned *birth rate* exceeds one per woman.

It may seem surprising that in the first stages of the transition when contraceptive use (intended to avoid unplanned pregnancies) rises rapidly, unplanned pregnancies

---

[4] This comparison ignores a small number of contraceptive failures.

are also rising. These trends are explained by the increasing difficulty women face in avoiding unplanned pregnancies as desired family size declines and countries move through the fertility transition. In pre- and early transitional countries most of women's reproductive years are required to bear wanted and planned children because desired family size is high. There are few unplanned pregnancies because there is little time at risk of such pregnancies. High rates of wanted fertility remove most reproductive years from the risk of unintended pregnancy.

In contrast, in countries at the end of the transition, with a desired family size near two, only a small proportion of the reproductive years is needed to bear two wanted children. Women then face the challenging task of avoiding unplanned pregnancies during the remaining reproductive years. When women desire just a few births during their childbearing years, the risk of unintended pregnancy is high, because of the many years during which pregnancy is not wanted. If women are sexually active both before and after the period of having wanted births, as most women are, they could face 20 or more years at risk of unplanned pregnancy. The rise in the number of years at risk of unplanned pregnancies over the course of the transition means that the period during which women must practice consistent and effective contraception lengthens considerably. In a hypothetical population with no practice of contraception or abortion and a desired family size of two, women can experience as many as 6 or 7 unplanned births in addition to the two wanted children.

An increase in contraceptive use and abortion offsets the upward pressure on unplanned pregnancies due to an increase in exposure over the course of the transition. Ideally there would be no unplanned pregnancies if all women who wish to avoid pregnancy use 100% effective contraception. In reality, few women are able to achieve this outcome. As discussed above, actual use falls short of demand even though both rise as the transition proceeds. The size of the gap between use and demand depends on the obstacles to contraceptive use identified above. As countries proceed through the transition, the obstacles typically decline, often aided by family planning programs. In addition, the opportunity costs of unintended births rise as women become more educated and have more flexible time because of fewer children, and able to earn an income in the market economy, thus leading to more careful and effective use of contraception. (Of course, the causal arrow also runs in the opposite direction: careful and effective use of contraception is a liberating force allowing women to more easily attain higher levels of education and higher rates of employment in the economy).

An additional factor contributing to substantial unplanned pregnancy rates especially in the later phases of the transition is the occasional failure of all contraceptive methods except sterilization.[5] A typical annual failure rate for pill users is 10% which implies a fifty percent failure rate in about seven years of use. Methods such as the IUD and implants have higher effectiveness, but the cumulative risk of an unplanned pregnancy over a decade or more is still substantial. The high level of unwanted births flowing from this substantial risk is reduced significantly by the use of abortion.

---

[5] Although, tubal sterilization is considered a permanent method of fertility control, pregnancy can occur in very rare cases.

In sum, any women who is sexually active and wants a small family has the difficult task of avoiding unplanned pregnancies during the many years she is at risk of conceiving. The transition in individual reproductive behavior entailed in moving to a small family norm requires a large increase in the level of birth control throughout the fecund years.

As countries move through their fertility transitions, the obstacles to consistent and effective birth control continue to be substantial for many women. As a result, the justification for public investment in low-cost access to high quality birth control extends into the later stages of fertility transition and persists even in post-transition societies. The key role of family planning programs in assisting women in implementing their reproductive preferences will be discussed in more detail in Chap. 7.

Appendix 1

Standard demographic methods are used to decompose the change in CPR into contributions made by changes in the demand for contraception and changes in the satisfaction of this demand (Das Gupta, 1993).

The following variables are used:

CPR   contraceptive prevalence among married/in union women.
D   Demand for contraception.
DS   Proportion of demand that is implemented.
ΔCPR   Change in CPR between first and last survey.
ΔCPRA   Component of ΔCPR attributable to change in demand between first and last survey.
ΔCPRB   Component of ΔCPR attributable to change in satisfaction between first and last survey.

By definition, CPR = D x DS.

Let the subscripts 1 and 2 refer, respectively, to the first and last available survey then the change in the CPR between the surveys is decomposed into its components by

$$\Delta CPR = \Delta CPRA + \Delta CPRB = \Delta D \times (DS1 + DS2)/2 + \Delta DS \times (D1 + D2)/2$$
$$\Delta CPRA = \Delta D \times (DS1 + DS2)/2$$
$$\Delta CPRB = \Delta DS \times (D1 + D2)/2$$

References

Bearak, J., Popinchalk, P., Ganatra, B., Moller, A., Tunçalp, O., Beavin, C., Kwok, L., & Alkema, L. (2020). Unintended pregnancy and abortion by income, region, and the legal status of abortion: Estimates from a comprehensive model for 1990–2019. *Lancet*. https://doi.org/10.1016/S2214-109X(20)30315-6

Bongaarts, J. (1984). Implications of future fertility trends for contraceptive practice. *Population and Development Review, 10*(2), 341–352.

Bongaarts, J. (2017). The effect of contraception on fertility: Is sub-Saharan Africa different? *Demographic Research, 37*(6), 129–146.

Bongaarts, J., & Bruce, J. (1995). The causes of unmet need for contraception and the social content of services. *Studies in Family Planning, 26*(2), 57–75.

Bongaarts, J., & Casterline, J. (2018). From fertility preferences to reproductive outcomes in the developing world. *Population and Development Review, 44*(4), 793–809.

Bongaarts, J., & Potter, R. (1983). *Fertility, biology and behavior: An analysis of the proximate determinants*. Academic.

Casterline, J., & Sinding, S. (2000). Unmet need for family planning in developing countries and implications for population policy. *Population and Development Review, 26*(4), 691–723.

Casterline, J., Perez, A., & Biddlecom, A. (1997). Factors underlying unmet need for family planning in the Philippines. *Studies in Family Planning, 28*(3), 173–191.

Casterline, J., Sathar, Z., & Ul Haque, M. (2001). Obstacles to contraceptive use in Pakistan: A study in Punjab. *Studies in Family Planning, 32*(2), 95–110.

Cleland, J., Bernstein, S., Ezeh, A., Faundes, A., Glasier, A., & Innis, J. (2006). Family planning: The unfinished agenda. *The Lancet, 368*(9549), 1810–1827.

Coale, A., & Watkins, S. (Eds.). (1986). *The decline of fertility in Europe*. Princeton University Press.

Das Gupta, P. (1993). Standardization and decomposition of rates: A user's manual, U.S. Bureau of the Census, Current Population Reports, Series P23–186, U.S. Government Printing Office.

El-Zanaty, F., Way, A., Kishor, S., & Casterline, J. (1999). *Egypt in-depth study on the reasons for nonuse of family planning*. National Population Council.

Feyisetan, B., & Casterline, J. B. (2000). Fertility preferences and contraceptive change In developing countries. *International Perspectives on Sexual and Reproductive Health, 26*(3),100–109.

Henry, L. (1961). Some data on natural fertility. *Eugenics Quarterly, 8*, 81–91.

Ibitoye, M., Casterline, J., & Zhang, C. (2022). Fertility preferences and contraceptive change in low-and middle-income countries. *Studies in Family Planning, 53*(2), 361–376.

ICF. (2021). The DHS Program STATcompiler. Retrieved September 29, 2021, from http://www.statcompiler.com.

Jain, A., Ross, J., Gribble, J., & McGinn, E. (2014). Inconsistencies in the total fertility rate and contraceptive prevalence rate in Malawi. Washington DC: Futures Group, Health Policy Project.

Johnston, R. (2021). Historical abortion statistics, ROK South Korea. https://www.johnstonsarchive.net/policy/abortion/ab-southkorea.html.

Knodel, J., & van de Walle, E. (1979). Lessons from the past: Policy implications of historical fertility studies. *Population and Development Review, 5*(2), 217–245.

Mauldin, W., & Segal, S. (1988). Prevalence of contraceptive use: Trends and issues. *Studies in Family Planning, 19*(6), 335–353. https://doi.org/10.2307/1966628.

Sedgh, G., Bearak, J., Singh, S., Bankole, A., Popinchalk, A., Ganatra, B., Rossier, C., Gerdts, C., Tunçalp, O., Johnson, B., Johnston, H., & Alkema, L. (2016). Abortion incidence between 1990 and 2014: global, regional, and subregional levels and trends. *Lancet, 388*(10041), 258–267.

Tsui, A. (2001). Population policies, family planning programs, and fertility: The record. *Population and Development Review, 27*(Supplement), 184–204.

United Nations. (2000). *Levels and trends of contraceptive use as assessed in 1998*. United Nations.

United Nations Population Division. (2019). World population prospects 2019, Online Edition. Rev.1. Department of Economic and Social Affairs, United Nations.

References

United Nations Population Division. (2021). *Estimates and projections of family planning indicators 2021*. United Nations.

Van de Walle, E. (1992). Fertility transition, conscious choice and numeracy. *Demography, 29*(4), 487–502.

Watkins, S. (1991). *From provinces into nations: Demographic integration in Western Europe, 1870–1960*. Princeton University Press.

Westoff, C., & Bankole, A. (2001). *The contraception-fertility link in sub-Saharan Africa and in other developing countries*. ORC Macro (DHS Analytical Studies No. 4).

Open Access This chapter is licensed under the terms of the Creative Commons Attribution 4.0 International License (http://creativecommons.org/licenses/by/4.0/), which permits use, sharing, adaptation, distribution and reproduction in any medium or format, as long as you give appropriate credit to the original author(s) and the source, provide a link to the Creative Commons license and indicate if changes were made.

The images or other third party material in this chapter are included in the chapter's Creative Commons license, unless indicated otherwise in a credit line to the material. If material is not included in the chapter's Creative Commons license and your intended use is not permitted by statutory regulation or exceeds the permitted use, you will need to obtain permission directly from the copyright holder.

Chapter 4
Socio-Economic Determinants of Fertility

4.1 Introduction

Conventional demographic and economic theories of the fertility transition emphasize the demand driven nature of reproductive change. These theories propose that socio-economic development raises the cost of children and reduces their benefits, thus leading parents to decrease their desired family size and to practice contraception or abortion to achieve lower fertility. A weakness of conventional theories about fertility transitions is its generality. Many socio-economic indicators such as GDP per capita, life expectancy, child survival, education, and urbanization are correlated with fertility in bivariate cross-sectional comparisons of countries, but for many decades there was no agreement on the dominant driver of fertility decline.

More recently, however, the extensive literature on this topic has increasingly emphasized the central role of education and especially women's education (Cleland, 2009; Cochrane, 1979; Gaylor, 2005; Hadden & London, 1996; Jejeebhoy, 1995; Kravdal, 2002; Lloyd, 2003; Lutz & Skirbekk, 2014; Murtin, 2013; Schultz, 1994; Summers, 1992a, 1992b). A comprehensive regression analysis of the determinants of fertility using time series of data from 1870 to 2000 by Murtin (2013) concludes that "…average years of primary schooling among the adult population, rather than income standards, child mortality, or total mortality rates, drive fertility down by about 40 percent to 80 percent when those years grow from zero (no literacy) to six years (full literacy). This result is robust to a variety of specifications, samples, and econometric models" (Murtin, 2013: 617). Similarly, Cleland (2009: 183) concludes: "Education of adults persistently emerges as the single most powerful predictor of their demographic behavior." Lutz and Skirbekk (2014: 15) agree: "…educational attainment is not just one of many socio-economic factors that matter…[it] is the single most important source of empirically observable population heterogeneity."

Several causes have been proposed for the effect of women's education on fertility, including greater autonomy in decision-making, more knowledge about reproduction and contraception, higher potential for earnings, and rising opportunity costs of childbearing (Diamond et al., 1999; Jejeebhoy, 1995; Lloyd, 2003). A related set of studies examines the role of mass schooling which may lower fertility in developing countries by reducing the children's potential to work in or outside the home, raising the costs of children, speeding up cultural change, and propagating middle-class values (Caldwell, 1980).

While there is a growing consensus about the key role of education as a cause of fertility decline, as well as about the minor roles of GDP per capita and percent urban, there is less agreement about the effect of child mortality. Several authors argue for a role of mortality decline as a determinant of fertility (Angeles, 2010; Canning et al., 2015; Cleland, 2001b), but others find little effect or point to methodological shortcomings of past studies thus leaving the question of the impact of mortality decline on fertility decline unresolved (Angeles, 2010; Murtin, 2013; Wolpin, 1998). It is possible that Notestein's original views, that mortality decline is a necessary but not sufficient condition for fertility decline and that social and economic changes are needed to bring about reproductive change, are correct (Notestein, 1945). The "necessary but not sufficient" hypothesis is consistent with the pattern observed in a number of the least developed contemporary Western African countries (e.g., Chad, Congo DR, Mali, and Niger), where child mortality has declined by half since the 1950s, but these improvements have only been followed by minor changes in fertility (United Nations, 2019).

This chapter begins by examining the evidence on the potential roles of several socio-economic variables as causes of fertility trends in the developing world from 1960 to 2015. The analysis confirms that female education is the dominant socio-economic driver of fertility transitions in the developing world. Next, a more in-depth examination of the fertility effects of education at different stages of the transitions reveals several unexpected findings, demonstrating that socio-economic changes alone provide only a partial and often inadequate explanation for fertility trends. The concluding section aims to explain these anomalies by resorting to diffusion theory, social influence, and family planning programs.

4.2 Data

The dependent variable in the regression analyses presented below is the total fertility rate. Estimates from 1960 to 2015 are taken from the United Nations fertility data base (United Nations Population Division, 2019). Other indicators such as the onset of the transition are derived from TFR trends (see Chap. 2).

The explanatory variables consist of the following country-level socio-economic indicators:

- Education, as measured by the average years of schooling among women aged 20–39 (Wittgenstein Center for Demography and Global Human Capital, 2015),[1]

---

[1] It should be emphasized that the number of years of schooling does not measure the quality of education.

- Child mortality, ages 0–4 (United Nations Population Division, 2019)
- Real GDP per capita (PPP[2]) taken from the Penn World Table (Feenstra et al., 2015)
- Percent of population that is urban (United Nations Population Division, 2018).

4.3 Which Socio-Economic Variable is the Main Driver of Fertility Transitions?

Population level fertility correlates with many socio-economic variables. To illustrate, Fig. 4.1 plots the 2015 cross-sectional relationship between the total fertility rate and four socio-economic indicators (womens' education, child mortality, GDP/capita, and percent urban) for 97 developing countries. All four correlations are in the expected direction and are highly statistically significant.

The key question now is whether these correlations are causal or simply due to collinearity. Answering this question requires a multivariate statistical analysis. We

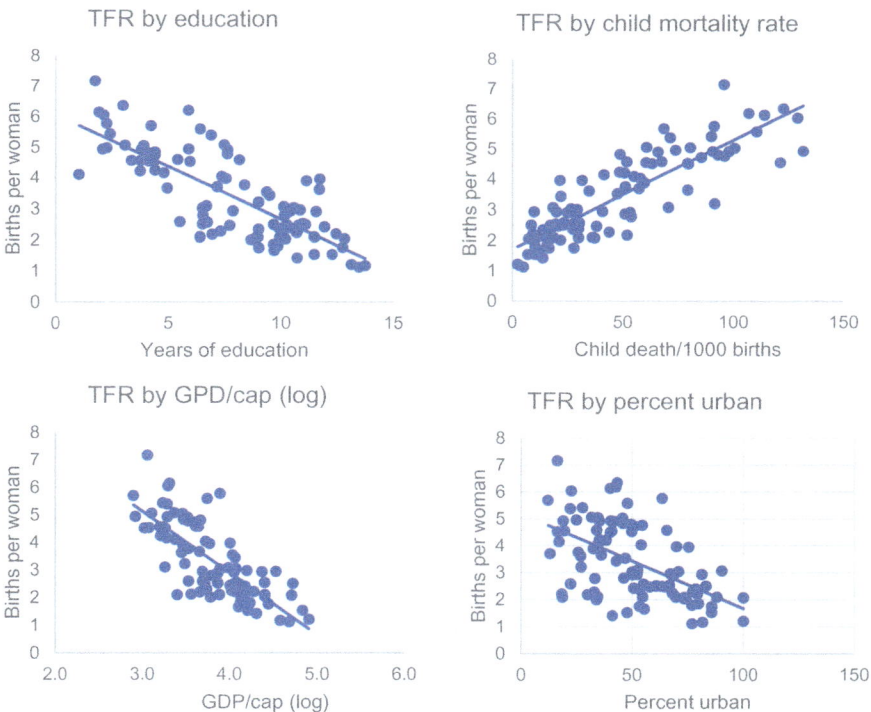

Fig. 4.1 Total fertility rate by socio-economic indicators for 97 developing countries in 2015

---

[2] PPP refers to purchasing power parity.

Table 4.1 Results of four fixed effects regression models with TFR as dependent variable. Data from 1960 to 2015

Dependent variable: total fertility rate				
	All countries		SS.Africa	Asia/NA/L.America
	Model 1	Model 2	Model 3	Model 4
Education	−0.42[a]	−0.41[a]	−0.35[a]	−0.38[a]
Child mortality	0.005[a]	0.005[a]	0.002[b]	0.008[a]
Log GDP/cap (PPP)	−0.001			
Percent urban	−0.001			
Constant	6.59	6.54	6.77	5.99
N	597	647	254	393
R^2	0.73	0.72	0.64	0.69

[a]$p < 0.001$, [b]$p < 0.01$, [c]$p < 0.05$, [d]$p < 0.1$

rely on fixed effect regression models which are the preferred approach when dealing with panel data such as we have with estimates of time series of the TFR and the explanatory variables for most countries from 1960 to 2015.

Table 4.1 presents the results of several such regressions in which the TFR is the dependent variable. Model 1 in this table summarizes the regression in which all four explanatory variables are included. The coefficients for education and child mortality are statistically significant ($p < 0.001$), while the effects of GDP/per capita and percent urban are not ($p > 0.1$). Model 2 represents the reduced model which drops these non-significant variables and again confirms that education and child mortality have a highly significant impact on fertility. Model 3 and 4 present the regional regression results for, respectively, SS.Africa and Asia/N.Africa/Latin America, with similar results except that the coefficient for child mortality is much smaller in SS.Africa than in Asia/N.Africa/L.America. The latter finding may be attributable in part to the AIDS epidemic which led to elevated levels of child mortality in much of SS.Africa after 1990.

The effect of education on the fertility level of a country can be estimated from the regression coefficient for education. For example, in model 1 this coefficient equals −0.42 which implies that an increase in years of education by 1 year leads on average to a decline in fertility of 0.42 births per woman. Similarly, a 10-year improvement in education would result in a decline of 4.2 births per women. The education coefficients for education in models 2, 3 and 4 are similar, although slightly smaller.

The regression coefficients presented in Table 4.1 are unstandardized. This means that their sizes cannot be usefully compared with one another because the variables are expressed in different units (e.g., years of education vs. child deaths per 1000 births). To assess which of the explanatory variables is most important as a determinant of fertility we calculated the standardized regression coefficients. In Model 2 for all countries the standardized coefficient equals 0.90 for education and 0.17 for child mortality (not shown in Table 4.1). This implies that education is five times more important than child mortality as an explanatory variable for fertility trends. The standardized regression coefficients for models 3 and 4 also show a dominance of education in SSAfrica (ninefold) and in Asia/N.Africa/L.America (threefold). Based on these findings we focus below on the effects of education on fertility transition patterns.

4.4 Education and Fertility Transition Patterns

Figure 4.2 plots trends in education (i.e., the number of years of schooling for women aged 20–39) for 97 developing countries from 1960 to 2015. As expected, large gains have been achieved since 1960 in almost all countries. Improvements in L.America and in Asia/N.Africa were most rapid with average years of schooling tripling from around three years to over nine years. Gains in SS.Africa were also substantial with the average education level moving from 0.9 to 5.4 years. Trends in individual countries are almost all smooth and steady, with a few exceptions due to crisis periods.

Classical demographic transition theory and other conventional theories of fertility change assume a direct link between development indicators and fertility. If a development indicator changes by a certain amount, then fertility is assumed to respond in a more-or-less predictable way. Given the smooth trends in education one would therefore expect relatively steady declines in fertility associated with improvements in education over the course of the transition.

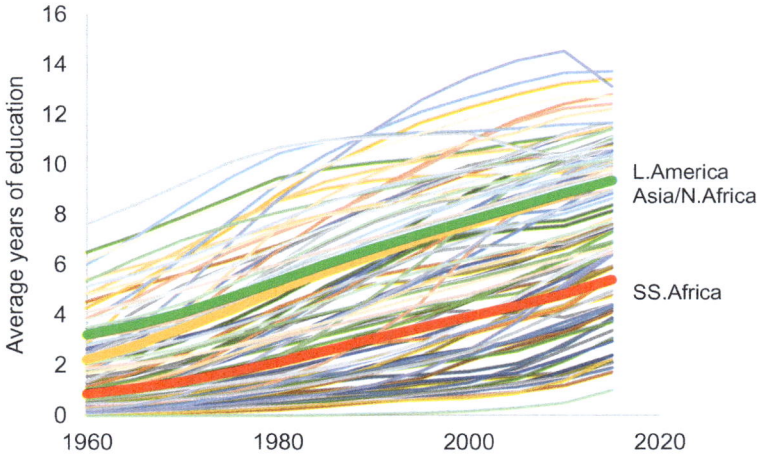

Fig. 4.2 Trends in education (years of schooling, women aged 20–39) from 1960 to 2015, 97 developing countries

Figure 4.3a–c examine this assumption. They present longitudinal trajectories of fertility by level of education for individual countries in the three major regions (only countries with a population size over 5 million are included). Each line in each figure represents the trajectory of one country with observations from 1960 to 2015. To simplify these figures, relative fertility (i.e., fertility as a proportion of maximum pre-transition fertility) is plotted to remove variation caused by differences in natural fertility.

As expected, in all regions the trend is one of declining fertility with rising education levels, but there is much variation in country trajectories. If education were the only determinant of fertility, then all countries would follow the same trajectory represented by the solid black regression line.[3] Any country's fertility level would solely be determined by its level of education and fluctuations in trends would solely be due to fluctuations in education. This clearly is not the case because a substantial proportion of variation in fertility is not explained by the level of education indicated by the regression line. For example, in SS.Africa the relative fertility of countries with 5 years of education ranges from 0.5 to 1.

Instead of random variations around a common trajectory over the course of the transition, clear patterns of deviation are visible. As the level education rises, fertility initially remains high and unchanged, followed by the transition's onset after which fertility declines rapidly through the middle of the transition. A slower pace of decline appears again near the transition's end as the country approaches replacement fertility.

There are several anomalies in the relationship between education and fertility. Such anomalies occur when the fertility response to a given increase in education is much larger or much smaller than expected. Most of these anomalies are evident in the panels of Fig. 4.3

Anomaly 1: **Before the onset of the transition fertility is unresponsive to increases in education**. In the first phase of a country's development process fertility typically remains high and unchanged as the education level improves. The duration of this flat section can last up eight years of education.

Anomaly 2: **The level of education at the onset of transitions ("the threshold") varies very widely among countries**. The education threshold for entering the transition ranges from a year or less in Ethiopia, Morocco and Haiti to as high as eight years for Tajikistan.

Anomaly 3: **The pace of change in fertility in mid-transition is faster than expected from the regression line**. This is the case even in a few countries with low levels of education (e.g., Bangladesh, Ethiopia, Morocco and Rwanda).

Anomaly 4: **Once a country in a region has entered the transition, neighboring countries follow suit even when they have lower levels of education**. The first countries to begin a sustained fertility decline within a region typically do so only after relatively high levels of education have been attained. Once a few countries have entered the transition, the threshold drops for the remaining countries and their

---

[3] Linear OLS regression lines are fitted to all data in the figure.

4.4 Education and Fertility Transition Patterns

Fig. 4.3 Relative fertility by years of education, 1960–2025, 59 developing countries with population size above 5 million

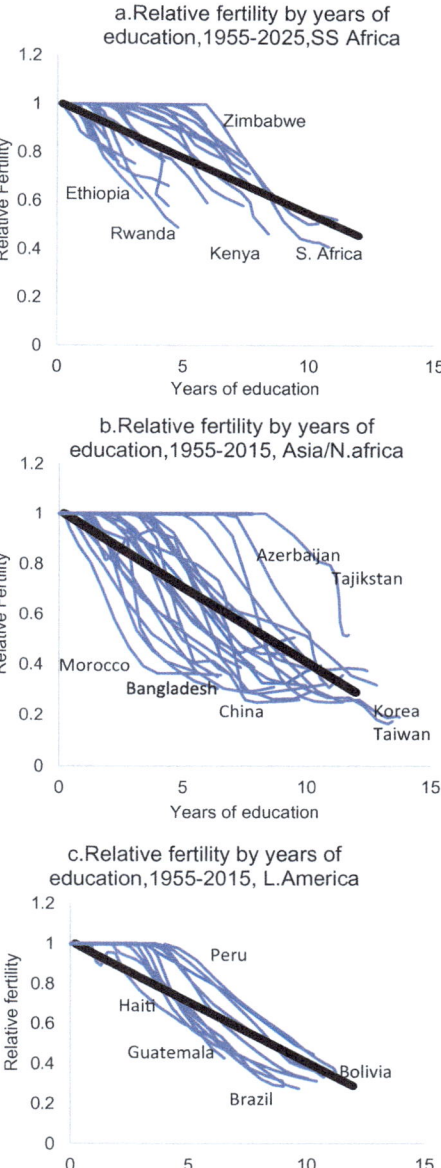

probability of entering a transition rises over time. The last countries to enter the transition have significantly lower levels of development than the region's "leaders." For example, in Asia levels of education in the early onset countries Korea and Taiwan were substantially higher than the threshold in Bangladesh and Pakistan. South Africa and Kenya started transitions at higher education levels than later transitions in Ethiopia, Malawi and Rwanda.

4.5 Explanations of Anomalies

The above anomalies have been documented in previous research in both historical European countries (Coale & Watkins, 1986) and in transitions in the developing world in recent decades (Bongaarts & Watkins, 1996; Cleland & Wilson, 1987). To explain these anomalies researchers have developed theories employing concepts that were neglected in conventional demographic theories: diffusion processes, social norms and family planning programs.

The *diffusion of innovations* refers to the process by which new information, technologies, ideas, behaviors, and attitudes spread within a population through a variety of mechanisms such as social networks, opinion leaders, and media (e.g., Bongaarts & Watkins, 1996; Casterline, 2001; Cleland, 2001a; Cleland & Wilson, 1987; Montgomery & Casterline, 1993, 1996; Rogers, 1973, 2003; Watkins, 1987). This spread is most rapid within linguistically and culturally homogeneous populations and it can be largely independent of social and economic changes. The closely related term of *social interaction* emphasizes the active role individuals can play in diffusing information by, for example, discussing new ideas and their benefits and costs.

Social norms and social influence refer to the effects that the views and beliefs of others have on an individual's behavior. An individual's behavior does not depend only on his or her characteristics, preferences and circumstances, but also on community norms. Deviating significantly from these norms carries a cost that most people try to avoid. Community institutions are designed in part to enforce these norms.

Family planning programs represent organized efforts by governments or NGOs to assist women with implementing their reproductive preferences and avoiding unplanned pregnancies. These goals are achieved in part by providing access to contraceptive methods and services. In addition, family planning programs undertake information and education campaigns to accelerate the diffusion of information about methods of contraception and about the costs and benefits of children thus contributing to a decline in desired family size. A more detailed discussion of the role of family planning programs is provided in Chap. 6.

These concepts help explain the anomalies identified in the previous section:

(1) *Pre-transitional fertility is not responsive to development.* In traditional patriarchal societies deviation from social norms is disapproved. This is an important

obstacle to the introduction of new behaviors such as contraceptive use in societies where it has been absent. As a result, the rise in education at the beginning of the development process initially leads to no change in fertility as women prefer not to deviate from traditions that support high fertility. Social influence thus acts initially as a constraint on the adoption of innovative behavior by individuals who prefer to limit childbearing.

(2) *The level of education at the onset of transitions ("the threshold") varies widely among countries.* As noted, threshold level of education ranges from less than one to eight years. The low thresholds in certain countries can be attributed to several factors. First, countries differ in their social resistance to new ideas, for example, due to conservative or religious traditions supporting high fertility and patriarchal family life. Second, countries differ greatly in the heterogeneity of their cultural, ethnic and linguistic composition. Ideas about contraception and the benefits of smaller families spread more rapidly in homogenous than in heterogeneous societies. Third, a country benefits from having earlier transitions in neighboring countries from which ideas might diffuse (see discussion below). Fourth, the early introduction of a government family planning program also accelerates the onset of transitions.

(3) *Rapid pace of decline in mid transition countries.* Several factors may be operating. First, the diffusion of information about methods of contraception and the costs and benefits of children can happen rapidly without much change in socio-economic conditions. Second, family planning programs accelerated the pace of the transition. Third, if the transition onset is delayed until a country has reached a relatively high level of education, there may be penned up demand for contraception, which can be implemented quickly thus leading to rapid fertility decline.

(4) *Once a country in a region has entered the transition, neighboring countries follow sooner than expected from their level of education.* This anomaly is a result of a decline over time in the threshold level of education at the onset of the transition. Figure 4.4 presents average education levels at the onset of the transition in successive decades by region. This threshold level has declined substantially over time. In the sixties and seventies, the onset of fertility occurred on average at about 4 years of education in Asia and L.America and above 5 years in SS Africa. But from the 1980s onward, transition onsets have occurred at substantially lower levels near two years. This trend is evident within each major region.

This moving threshold would likely not occur if countries were isolated from one another. However, countries are linked through a variety of channels of social interaction: personal and institutional links exists among communities within the same country and among countries, facilitating diffusion and social interaction. Consequently, as time goes by, the probability of entering the transition rises for those communities and countries that have not yet done so. For example, Bangladesh was one of the last countries in Asia to enter its fertility transition and therefore had many regional examples of countries where transitions were already underway (e.g., Korea, Taiwan, Malaysia). These earlier transitions

Fig. 4.4 Average years of education at transition onset by region and decade of onset

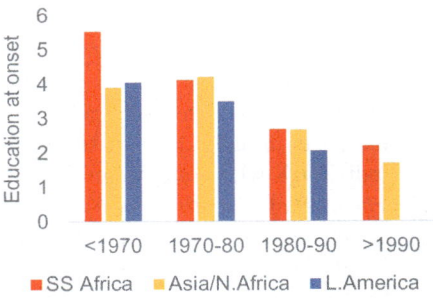

in neighboring countries demonstrated to governments that family planning programs could be successful.

An interesting implication of this declining threshold is that the difference in the timing of transitions between early- and late-starting countries in a given region is reduced from many decades to just two or three. For example, Bangladesh's transition would have been delayed by several decades if it had to wait until it achieved the same level of development as Taiwan and Korea had in 1960. Because of the moving threshold, transition onsets in Asia/N.Africa and Latin America have been concentrated in the 1960 and 1970s and in the 1980 and 1990s for SS Africa.

In sum, before the transition onset, social norms can inhibit fertility change. But once innovative fertility behavior has been adopted by a group of individuals within a community, by a community within a country, or by a few countries within a region, norms change and social interaction can become a powerful force that stimulates its onset elsewhere and accelerates the pace of transition in the rest of the community, the nation, or the world. Family planning programs accelerate all these processes.

References

Angeles, L. (2010). Demographic transitions: Analyzing the effects of mortality on fertility. *Journal of Population Economics, 23*(1), 99–120.

Bongaarts, J., & Watkins, S. (1996). Social interactions and contemporary fertility transitions. *Population and Development Review, 22*(4), 639–682.

Caldwell, J. (1980). Mass education as a determinant of the timing of fertility decline. *Population and Development Review, 6*(2), 225–255.

Canning, D., Raja, S., & Yazbeck, A. (2015). *Africa's demographic transition: Dividend or disaster?* World Bank Group.

Casterline, J. (2001). Diffusion processes and fertility transition: Introduction. In J. B. Casterline (Ed.), *Diffusion processes and fertility transition: Selected perspectives* (pp. 1–77). Committee on Population, Division of Behavioral and Social Sciences and Education, National Research Council. National Academy Press.

References

Cleland, J. (2001a) Potatoes and pills: An overview of innovation-diffusion contributions to explanations of fertility decline. In J. B. Casterline (Ed.), *Diffusion processes and fertility transition: Selected perspectives* (pp. 39–65). National Academy Press.

Cleland, J. (2001b). The effects of improved survival on fertility: A reassessment. In R. A. Bulatao & J. B. Casterline (Eds.), *Global fertility transition. Population and Development Review 27*(Suppl.), 60–92.

Cleland, J. (2009). Education and future fertility trends, with special reference to mid-transitional countries. In *Completing the fertility transition* (pp. 183–194). United Nations Population Bulletin, Special Issue Nos. 48/49 (2002).

Cleland, J., & Wilson, C. (1987). Demand theories of the fertility decline: An iconoclastic view. *Population Studies, 41*(1), 5–30.

Coale, A., & Watkins, S. (Eds.). (1986). *The decline of fertility in Europe*. Princeton University Press.

Cochrane, S. (1979). *Fertility and education: What do we really know?* Johns Hopkins University Press.

Diamond, I., Newby, M., & Varle, S. (1999). Female education and fertility: Examining the links. In C. Bledsoe, J. B. Casterline, J. Johnson-Kuhn & J. Haaga (Eds.), *Critical perspectives on schooling and fertility in the developing world. Committee on population* (pp. 23–48). Commission on Behavioral and Social Sciences and Education, National Research Council, National Academy Press.

Feenstra, R., Inklaar, R., & Timmer, M. (2015). The next generation of the penn world table. *American Economic Review, 105*(10), 3150–3182. www.ggdc.net/pwt.

Gaylor, O. (2005). The demographic transition and the emergence of sustained economic growth. *Journal of the European Economic Association, 3*(2–3), 494–504.

Hadden, K., & London, B. (1996). Educating girls in the third world. *International Journal of Comparative Sociology, 37*(1–2), 31–46.

ICF International. (2019). The DHS Program STAT compiler. https://www.statcompiler.com.

Jejeebhoy, S. (1995). *Women's education, autonomy, and reproductive behaviour: Experience from developing countries*. Clarendon Press.

Kravdal, O. (2002). Education and fertility in sub-Saharan Africa: Individual and community effects. *Demography, 39*(2), 233–250.

Lloyd, C. (2003). Education. In Demeny, P. & McNicoll, G. (Eds.). (2003). *Encyclopedia of population* (pp. 278–283). Macmillan.

Lutz, W., & Skirbekk, V. (2014). How education drives demography and knowledge informs projections. In W. Lutz, W. P. Butz, & K. C. Samir (Eds.), *World population and human capital in the twenty-first century* (pp. 14–38). Oxford University Press.

Montgomery, M., & Casterline, J. (1993). The diffusion of fertility control in Taiwan: Evidence from pooled cross-section time-series models. *Population Studies, 47*(3), 457–479.

Montgomery, M., & Casterline, J. (1996). Social learning, social influence, and new models of fertility. In J. B. Casterline, R. D. Lee & K. A. Foote (Eds.), *Fertility in the United States: New patterns, new theories. Population and Development Review 22*(Suppl.), 151–175.

Murtin, F. (2013). Long-term determinants of the demographic transition, 1870–2000. *The Review of Economics and Statistics, 95*(2), 617–631.

Notestein, F. (1945) Population: The long view. In T. Schultz (Ed.), *Food for the world* (pp. 36–57). University of Chicago Press.

Rogers, E. (1973). *Communication strategies for family planning*. Free Press.

Rogers, E. (2003). *Diffusion of innovations*. Free Press.

Schultz, P. (1994). Human capital, family planning and their effects on population growth. *American Economic Review, 84*(2), 255–260.

Summers, L. (1992a). Investing in all the people. *The Pakistan Development Review, 31*(4), 367–404.

Summers, L. (1992b). The most influential investment. *Scientific American*, 132

United Nations Population Division. (2018). *World urbanization prospects: The 2018 revision*. Online Edition.

United Nations Population Division. (2019). *World population prospects: The 2019 revision*. United Nations.

Watkins, S. (1987). The fertility transition: Europe and the third world compared. *Sociological Forum, 2*(4), 645–673.

Wittgenstein Centre for Demography and Global Human Capital. (2015). Wittgenstein Centre Data Explorer Version 1.2. http://www.wittgensteincentre.org/dataexplorer.

Wolpin, K. (1998). The impact of infant and child mortality risk on fertility. In M. R. Montgomery & B. Cohen (Eds.), *From death to birth: Mortality decline and reproductive change* (pp. 74–111). The National Academies Press.

Open Access This chapter is licensed under the terms of the Creative Commons Attribution 4.0 International License (http://creativecommons.org/licenses/by/4.0/), which permits use, sharing, adaptation, distribution and reproduction in any medium or format, as long as you give appropriate credit to the original author(s) and the source, provide a link to the Creative Commons license and indicate if changes were made.

The images or other third party material in this chapter are included in the chapter's Creative Commons license, unless indicated otherwise in a credit line to the material. If material is not included in the chapter's Creative Commons license and your intended use is not permitted by statutory regulation or exceeds the permitted use, you will need to obtain permission directly from the copyright holder.

Chapter 5
Controversies Surrounding Fertility Policies

5.1 Introduction

What is the relationship between development and fertility decline? Is Path 1 (Fig. 1.4), socio-economic development, the cause of the developing world's fertility transition? Can Path 2, family planning programs, stimulate fertility decline in agrarian societies and thereby expedite economic development? Can the causal arrow between development and fertility decline run both ways? Many of the controversies surrounding the developing world's fertility transition centered on these questions. They sound like dry "academic" questions, but they played out in a contentious international political environment during the decades following WWII.

The spread of an effective vaccine for smallpox, the use of newly developed antibiotics, and the application of effective methods for controlling malaria produced unprecedented mortality decline at mid-century. Between 1950 and 1970 life expectancy (United Nations, 2019) increased by 25% for the world, 33% for Asia, 20% for Latin America and the Caribbean, and 25% for Africa. Since the developing world's fertility declined little during this period (see Fig. 1.1), rates of population growth increased, especially in Asia and Africa. Fears of famine and stagnant economic growth grew. The First Five Year Plan (1951) of newly independent India noted this connection (Paragraph 105): "The recent increase in the population of India and the pressure exercised on the limited resources of the country have brought to the forefront the urgency of the problem of family planning and population control." Funds were allocated to establish a "family planning programme" in the Ministry of Health and Family Welfare. As early as 1958 Sweden began a pilot family planning project in Ceylon aimed at lowering birth rates (Hyrenius and Åhs, 1968).

Colonial empires crumbled and political independence brought rising expectations and a universal quest for development. In the postwar bi-polar world the United States and the Soviet Union vied for the allegiance of Third World countries whose hopes and problems became a matter of concern to First World policymakers and academics. The "uncommitted" third of the world was a "prize" to be won in a struggle between "the Communist and the free worlds" (Davis, 1956: 354). Demographer Philip Hauser worried in *Science* (Hauser, 1960: 1646) that "explosive population growth" would frustrate the development plans of "underdeveloped nations" and expose them to the "blandishments" of the Communist bloc. He feared that "if the underdeveloped Communist nations demonstrate that they can achieve more rapid economic progress than the underdeveloped free nations, the free way of life may well be doomed. Success or failure in this fateful contest may well hinge on the ability of the nations involved to decrease their rates of population growth." The Cold War, as well as genuine humanitarian concerns, obliged policymakers and academics to look at fertility decline, the only humane way of decreasing the developing world's population growth, in a new way (Hodgson, 1988).

5.2 Controversies During the Pre-transition Phase, 1950–1970

In the mid-1940s demographers at Princeton University outlined a theory explaining modern demographic trends. Transition theory viewed all trends in mortality, fertility, and population growth as being responses to structural changes associated with "modernization". A society transforming from a traditional agrarian state to a modern industrial one would first experience mortality decline as people quickly employed increased production to improve diets, housing, and health. When significant numbers found themselves in competitive jobs living in cities and faced with the costs of children increasing and their economic benefits declining, small families became the norm. The period of rapid population growth brought on by the early decline of mortality came to an end when fertility approached mortality's low level in fully modernized societies.

In cases where a traditional agrarian society suffered colonial domination, transition theorists (Davis, 1945: 5–11; Kirk, 1944: 28–35; Notestein, 1945: 50–57; Thompson, 1946: 251–318) contended that an attenuated, "one-sided" modernization caused a peculiar demographic imbalance. Colonial domination produced the rationalization and commercialization of agriculture, the maintenance of internal order, improvements in transportation and communication, and the implementation of public health innovations, all of which resulted in mortality decline. Yet colonial rule prevented or failed to foster, the urbanization and industrialization that were expected to lower fertility. Thompson (1946: 313) called this "the Malthusian dilemma of all colonialism" and predicted the demise of the colonial system.

Some observers in colonies came to the same conclusions. In 1947 A. R. Paterson, Director of Medical Services of Kenya Colony, presented evidence of rapidly declining mortality, estimating a 2 to 2.3% annual rate of population growth. The British presence, he contended, so positively affected health conditions that it ignited "the time fuse of a biological bomb." The response of Africans, he feared, to "any

5.2 Controversies During the Pre-transition Phase, 1950–1970

direct birth-control propaganda would merely be 'Now indeed, we know that your object is to exterminate us'" (Paterson, 1947: 147). In the end he reasoned that only a program of industrialization and modernization would stimulate a desire for smaller families. Well before that could happen, however, the Mau Mau rebellion erupted in Kenya and independence came in 1963.

Myrdal (1970: 153) noted that "the population explosion has been by far the most important social and economic change in the underdeveloped countries in recent decades." Although it was widely recognized that rapid population growth would inhibit development in the poorest countries, there was initially no consensus on how to address the problem. This lack of agreement led to vigorous academic and policy debates.

5.2.1 *From Transition Theory to Advocacy of Family Planning Programs*

In the 1950s demographers found themselves in a perplexing situation. They faced what they believe was a crisis with a theory about demographic transitions that argued that modernization propelled changes in fertility and mortality, and offered little support for the idea that a "direct" family planning approach would work to change women's reproductive behavior. Notestein in his original version of demographic transition theory contended that fertility control was determined by social structural factors. Change the social structure with "a complete and integrated program of modernization," and fertility would decline, "for it is only when rising levels of living, improved health, increasing education, and rising hope for the future give new value to the individual life that old customs break and fertility comes under control" (Notestein, 1945: 57). Yet just eight years later, in the face of increasing rates of population growth, he saw "almost insuperable difficulties involved in achieving the sort of economic development required to permit reliance upon the automatic processes of social-economic change for the transition to low birth- and death-rates" (1953: 25). He described the new situation (Notestein, 1953: 25): "The objective is no longer restricted to the increase of production. It now also becomes that of speeding the processes of social change in directions that yield falling birth-rates, which in turn will permit more rapid increases in per capita income." To resolve this dilemma, he went on to advocate trying "direct measures" to lower fertility: "It is within the bounds of possibility that the wise use of modern methods of communication and training to promote higher marriage age and the practice of birth control would bring a considerable reduction of the birth-rate even in peasant societies" (Notestein, 1953: 28).

Kingsley Davis and other population scientists underwent a similar change during that decade (Hodgson, 1983). In 1945 Davis thought that "the Asiatic peoples, and others as well, will acquire modern civilization in time to check their fertility and thus achieve an efficient demographic balance" (1945: 10). Yet only a year later

Davis was calling "rapid and massive population growth" India's "gravest problem," noting that economic development could not "indefinitely provide for increasing numbers" (Davis, 1946: 243). By 1950 population growth had become the independent variable in Davis' thinking and development the dependent one (1950a: 43): "Can industrialization of the underdeveloped areas be achieved in face of their population problem?" His answer was stark: first there is likely to be "strife and turmoil, which at once reduce the existing demographic glut and sweep away old institutions and vested interests" (1950a: 49). By 1953 he was somewhat more optimistic about birth control, contending that if only new birth control technologies could be developed and governments would use the means at their disposal to construct effective family planning programs "the results may prove astounding to the skeptics" (Davis, 1953: 19). He saw "no inherent reason why peasant-agrarian populations cannot adopt the customs of fertility control, in advance of and to the advantage of modern economic development" (Davis, 1953: 18).

Both Davis and Notestein questioned the predictive ability of demographic transition theory's modernization explanation of fertility decline. In 1953 Notestein presented a standard version of transition theory but then followed with an equally lengthy consideration of apparent exceptions to the transition model, including the birth rate declines in eighteenth century agrarian France and more recently in Bulgaria, an "almost wholly agricultural area." He concluded that the rise of urban-industrial society "provided no mystical means for the reduction of fertility" (Notestein, 1953: 18). Likewise in 1954 Davis questioned the validity and utility of transition theory. He began by asking about the Western experience and how accurate the theory had been "as a description of fact." He noted that the length of the transition period from high to low vital rates had varied greatly among Western countries. He also pointed out that the magnitude and contour of the gap between mortality and fertility decline had exhibited no universal pattern. Finally, he emphasized that the West's increase in fertility since the mid-1930s cast doubt that a transition had been completed or a "cycle" terminated. He concluded: "Clearly the notion of the demographic transition, despite its fruitfulness as an organizing idea, should not be viewed as inevitable or as a predictive instrument" (Davis, 1954: 67–68). Later research under the direction of Coale (1969: 18) examined the historical relationship between the timing of marital fertility decline in a number of European countries and found there "to be little in the statistical record for Europe which confirms the existence of an association between the beginning of fertility decline and any specific level, or threshold, of economic and social development."

While demographers debated the strengths and weaknesses of demographic transition theory, the focus of policy makers increasingly turned to the option of direct intervention to lower fertility by means of family planning programs. But policy makers needed some evidence to support the feasibility of Path 2 (Fig. 1.4), family planning, as a way to achieve needed fertility declines. As early as 1950 Kingsley Davis interpreted the findings of a survey of rural Indian women as offering such evidence. Responders expressed a modal preference for a woman of forty having two or three living children, an answer which Davis construed as "a desire among Indian peasants for small families" (Davis, 1950b: 17). The implications of such findings were obvious. If a "ready market" for birth control could be demonstrated, then a family planning approach to fertility decline appeared feasible. Surveys of knowledge, attitudes, and practices with regard to family planning matters (KAP studies) were administered in a wide variety of settings. By 1970 four hundred KAP surveys had been conducted in virtually all of the world's geographic and cultural areas (Fawcett, 1970: 38). Although criticized for being "methodologically naïve" (Hauser, 1967: 404), these surveys collected data which could be interpreted to mean that a substantial majority of respondents were interested in learning methods of fertility control. KAP studies supplied to those working within the family planning movement their most powerful weapon with which to combat the doubts raised by decades of prior social demographic research that suggested fertility decline was invariably linked to modernization.

In the mid-1940s demographers studying fertility transitions had been able to differentiate industrialized, industrializing, and non-industrialized societies on the basis of the presence and extent of their fertility declines. The close relationship between the level of economic development and the level of fertility had been considered confirmation of their contention that Path 1 (Fig. 1.4), socio-economic development, led to lower mortality and lower desired family size and explained the fertility transition. During the 1950 and 1960s advocates of the new "direct approach" to fertility decline were able to classify individuals within a given population into users of contraception, potential users, and nonusers. The existence of a sizable group of potential users was considered confirmation that family planning programs, Path 2, could play a central role in bringing about the developing world's fertility transition.

Further support for investments in family planning programs came during the 1950s from economists who quantified the economic gains that a decline in fertility might entail. They emphasized the role played by capital accumulation in the development process. Underdevelopment represented a workforce with little capital stock, and development was a process of adding to that stock. Rapid population growth produced high dependency ratios that increased the need for "demographic investments" and thereby limited the capital available for more directly productive investments. Some theorists (Leibenstein, 1954; Nelson, 1956) developed models describing a "low-level equilibrium trap" in which population growth stymied growth of per capita income. The specter of growing numbers living at subsistence levels, making economic development increasingly improbable, was presented as a real possibility (Leibenstein, 1954: 70, 194). Coale and Hoover (1958) quantified the economic cost of continued high fertility and found it significant. This research in particular was used to convince developing world leaders of the benefits of fertility control and slower population growth.

5.2.2 The Rise of a Population Control Movement

The concerns of a small group of American demographers would have meant little if they had not been amplified by the actions of certain wealthy individuals and foundations that also worried about the geo-political significance of developing world demographic trends. During the early 1950s, John D. Rockefeller 3rd and the leadership of the Ford and Rockefeller foundations worked to establish a neo-Malthusian movement with a global focus. Their goal was to establish family planning programs throughout the developing world, lower fertility, and lessen population growth. They recognized that only governments could implement effective family planning programs, and their immediate task became convincing government leaders, in both developed and developing countries, that high fertility and rapid population growth were major social problems in need of state intervention. They determined that a dramatic increase in academic research on international population issues was a necessary first step in this conversion process. During the next two decades they expended millions of dollars to develop demographic research centers that focused on international population issues as well as on bio-medical research to develop new contraceptives.

The expenditures on demographic research had a profound impact. In the United States in 1950, for example, courses in demography could be found at the graduate level in only three universities. Between 1951 and 1967 major population research centers were established at 16 US universities; all owed their existence to foundation funding, largely from the Ford Foundation. Similar expenditures helped to establish internationally oriented population centers at a number of major universities in Europe and Australia. Funding from the Population Council, a research and technical assistance organization established by John D. Rockefeller 3rd in 1952 to provide a leadership role for the international population control movement, helped establish UN regional centers for demographic training and research in Bombay, India (1957), Santiago, Chile (1958), and Cairo, Egypt (1963). Additionally, its fellowship program brought hundreds of developing world students to major population research centers in developed countries for graduate training in demography.

The international population movement experienced heady times in the 1960s. In March 1963 the Ford Foundation trustees stated their intention to "maintain strong efforts both in the United States and abroad to achieve breakthroughs on the problems of population control" (Harkavy, 1995: 39). That same year the Rockefeller Foundation population program announced their bold goal to "bring about reduction of the growth rate of the world's population and its eventual stabilization" (Harkavy, 1995: 44). Such a goal became more credible with the conversion of previously reluctant First World governments to neo-Malthusianism. In January 1965 President Johnson (1965a) endorsed international family planning programs in his State of the Union message, promising to "seek new ways to use our knowledge to help deal with the explosion in world population and the growing scarcity in world resources." That year USAID began providing technical assistance in family planning, with President Johnson (1965b) presenting an economic argument for family planning: "Let us act on the fact that less than $5 invested in population control is worth $100 invested in economic growth." When he (Johnson, 1966: 321) first asked Congress for fertility control funds, he did so on the basis that high population growth rates "challenge our own security."

The US government immediately began to expend significant funds on fertility control. Department of Health, Education, and Welfare expenditures increased from $4.6 million in 1965 to $14.7 million in 1969; USAID funding increased from $10.5 million in 1965 to $45.4 million in 1969 and to $123 million by 1972 (Caldwell & Caldwell, 1986: 102–104). Most of the funds came to flow through the Office of Population at USAID, which due to the convictions of Dr. Reimert Ravenholt, its director, were spent on family planning programs to maximize their immediate impact on fertility (Warwick, 1982: 45–51). The involvement of the US government politicized the population control movement, especially since the US simultaneously was ramping up its unpopular involvement in the Vietnam conflict. In much of the Third World the US came to be seen as having its own agenda for the newly independent nations that might not correspond with their own desires.

There was also significant international involvement in developing world family planning happening at the same time (Caldwell, 2002: 3–4). In 1965 the World Health Organization entered the field, and family planning advisory commissions were sent to India by both the World Bank and the United Nations. That same year the IUSSP and UN Population Division organized a World Population Conference in Belgrade. In 1967, at the instigation of the Secretary-General of the United Nations, the UN Trust Fund for Population Activities was established to fund family planning programs; its name changed to the UN Fund for Population Activities in 1969. In 1950 the UN Population Division had projected that the world's population would reach 3.3 billion by 1980, but by 1968 their projection for that year had increased to a much more accurate 4.5 billion. Rapid population growth had become a significant global concern.

5.2.3 Fears of Famine, Failure and a Population Bomb

In the 1950 and 1960s India and China, densely settled and with rapidly increasing populations, both experienced significant challenges to their development efforts. Questions arose about food shortages and mass starvation. From 1958 to 1962 China attempted a "Great Leap Forward," an accelerated industrialization effort. Mao Zedong launched this campaign to quickly move China from an agrarian economy to a communist industrial one through the formation of people's communes that would dramatically increase grain yields and simultaneously bring industry to the countryside. It failed miserably. Grain production dropped significantly leading to tens of millions of starvation deaths, which were systematically hidden from view. And the small backyard steel furnaces produced very little useable steel.

India's major challenge in 1965 was growing enough food to feed its 500 million people, increasing at more than 2% a year. Since independence India had experience a number of famines and between 1954 and 1965 the US had granted it $30 billion worth of agricultural assistance (Ahlberg, 2007: 673). In 1965 the US shipped 20% of the its entire wheat harvest to India to make up its growing grain deficit. With the US grain surplus shrinking, mass starvation seemed imminent. In

1966, as India was experiencing a drought that threatened famine for 77 million people, President Johnson told Indian officials that the US would withhold its wheat shipments unless India "modernized" its agriculture and enhanced its family planning efforts (Ahlberg, 2007: 695). Under this US pressure India did fit more women with new IUDs, some causing significant infections (Connelly, 2008: 220–223). And throughout its prime wheat growing areas it planted the dwarf variety of wheat that Norman Borlaug, with Rockefeller Foundation funding, had perfected just four years earlier. The dwarf variety required the extensive use of irrigation, fertilizers, pesticides, and mechanization. This "Green Revolution" produced a record 1968 wheat crop that simultaneously put India on the road to food self-sufficiency and began a process that made redundant a significant portion of India's agriculture workforce.

During the 1960s doubts surfaced over whether voluntary family planning programs (Path 2) could produce the fertility decline needed to adequately control population growth. Davis (1967) now argued that to bring growth rates to sustainable levels, state interventions much more intrusive than providing couples with contraceptives would be needed, measures such as increasing the permissible age of marriage, paying people to be sterilized, or levying a "child tax" on parents. Hardin (1968), with his evocative image of the Commons, provided the rationale for moving "beyond family planning": pursuit of individual goals can, at times, work against the collective interest. Those believing that high fertility significantly worsened the commonweal thought governments might have the right (perhaps the duty) to limit individual reproductive freedom. In the 1970s both China and India responded to their experiences by implementing coercive fertility control programs.

Norman Borlaug won the 1970 Nobel Peace prize for developing high-yield cereal strains that helped feed the world's hungry people. In his acceptance speech (Borlaug, 1970) he noted that "there can be no permanent progress in the battle against hunger until the agencies that fight for increased food production and those that fight for population control unite in a common effort." He viewed his accomplishment as providing a short breathing space during which the "population monster" might be subdued. Others thought that such a "breathing space" no longer existed. In 1967 William and Paul Paddock, agronomist and diplomat respectively, published *Famine 1975! America's Decision: Who Will Survive?* Their analysis (Paddock & Paddock, 1967) of recent famines led them to believe that population growth was placing many developing countries on a collision course with starvation, and they outlined a triage approach for the US to use with its limited grain surplus. It would block all food aid to countries deemed incapable of ever achieving food self-sufficiency. In his review of the Paddocks' book in *Science*, James Bonner, a Caltech plant biologist, found (Bonner, 1967: 915) that "all responsible investigators agree that the tragedy will occur," differing only on "whether it will take place in ten years or less, or in ten years or a little more."

A year later Paul Ehrlich published his widely read Malthusian tract, *The Population Bomb* (Ehrlich, 1968), that identified overpopulation as the fundamental cause of not only famine in the developing world but of global environmental deterioration. By 1970 over 88% of Americans believed that the world was experiencing a population problem, and over 70% thought that the United States was also

(Westoff & McCarthy, 1979). In 1972 the Commission on Population Growth and the American Future, appointed by President Nixon and headed by John D. Rockefeller 3rd, issued a fundamentally neo-Malthusian report (Commission on Population Growth, 1972) recommending "that the nation welcome and plan for a stabilized population."

Although the apocalyptic views of the Paddocks, Ehrlich and others were not universally accepted there was wide agreement that rapid population growth was a serious problem that deserved to be high on the international policy agenda. Family planning programs were considered an important intervention that should be fully supported by governments everywhere. China's and India's coercive programs inevitably produced strong national and international criticism that affected all discussions of population policy for the next several decades. The large majority of developing countries, however, considered coercion unacceptable and implemented voluntary family planning programs.

5.3 Controversies During the Rapid Decline Phase, 1970–2000

5.3.1 *Controversy at the 1974 UN Conference on Population*

By the time the UN held its World Population Conference at Bucharest in 1974 advocacy of population control had come to be identified as a First World policy position. Like "the links of a food chain" (Notestein 1971: 82), the actions of a few concerned and influential individuals in the United States led to the involvement of foundations, universities, governments, and finally international organizations in this effort. Many voices carried the message: the World Bank, USAID, a number of Western governments, a variety of United Nations agencies, economists and demographers trained in Western universities, to name a few. And Third World governments could easily find First World monetary support for fertility control (Piotrow, 1973: 145–158). This raised questions about motives and priorities.

Those initiating the conference, principally the United States, planned it to be a staging ground for a united worldwide effort to lower fertility through voluntary family planning programs (Finkle & Crane, 1975: 87). Yet the "world" divided. The head of the Indian delegation asserted "development is the best contraceptive" and was greeted with "the acclaim of most Third World participants" (Ford Foundation, 1985: 18). This slogan questioned the priorities of First World actors, not the usefulness of family planning programs for individuals. The view that continued underdevelopment, unemployment, and malnutrition were fundamentally caused by rapid population growth had great attraction to First World policymakers, and family planning programs seemed a relatively inexpensive way to mitigate these problems. The view that underdevelopment, unemployment, malnutrition, and rapid population growth were fundamentally caused by the ties of dependency that bound the Third

World to the developed world had great attraction to Third World policymakers, but ending these ties would require crafting a difficult "new international economic order." Few Third World leaders at Bucharest, even those with active family planning programs, could resist making political points about the misplaced priorities of the United States (Finkle & Crane, 1975: 109). The conference ended with the adoption of a developmentalist World Population Plan of Action, and with John D. Rockefeller 3rd (Rockefeller, 1974: 4) announcing his conversion: "I now strongly believe that the only viable course is to place population policy solidly within the context of general economic and social development."

This developmentalist position was a challenge to the population control movement: assuming that development and fertility control could proceed hand in hand assumed a population problem significantly less virulent than the one perceived at mid-century. Although clearly a political defeat for the movement, it is not clear that the Bucharest Plan of Action had a noticeable effect on the course of the developing world's fertility transition. By 1974 evidence of fertility decline was appearing in many developing countries. Significant numbers had already begun their fertility transitions (Fig. 2.2). Singapore had completed its transition, and South Korea, Mauritius, and China would do so within a decade (Fig. 2.4). Two years after the Bucharest conference the UN first surveyed governments about their population policy positions (Table 5.1). Of the 116 developing countries responding, 55 countries, with 79% of the developing world's population, reported that they thought their fertility level was "too high." Forty countries, with 77% of the developing world's population, reported that they had a policy to lower fertility. And seventy-four countries, with 87% of the developing world's population, claimed to offer "direct support" for family planning services, implying that family planning services were being "provided through government-run facilities or outlets," although no data was collected on how extensive these provisions of services were.

Clearly, the precepts of the population control movement, that fertility levels were too high and needed to be lowered, had made significant inroads among developing country governments by the mid-1970s. The move to coercive population control by China and India during the 1970s, two of the loudest critics of the US at Bucharest, convincingly showed that they too believed that lower fertility was needed. The responses to the UN's follow-up 1986 and 1996 surveys (Table 5.1) indicate a continuous increase in governments' adopting antinatalist policies and providing direct support for family planning. By 1996 nine developing countries had already completed their fertility transitions, and some of them, including China, had shifted their view of fertility from "too high" to "satisfactory."

By the mid-1970s African countries, though, had yet to embrace the need for fertility control. Only three African countries (Tunisia, Morocco, and South Africa) had started their fertility transitions by 1974. Of the forty-eight African countries responding to the 1976 UN population policy survey (Table 5.2), eighteen, with 35% of Africa's population, thought that their fertility was "too high." Only twelve countries, with 30% of Africa's population, had a policy to lower fertility. There were historical reasons for African countries' hesitancy to view high fertility and rapid population growth as problematic. Many countries had only recently emerged

5.3 Controversies During the Rapid Decline Phase, 1970–2000

Table 5.1 UN world population policy survey 1976, 1986, 1996: developing world

	Number of countries			Percent of countries			Percent of population in developing world		
	1976	1986	1996	1976	1986	1996	1976	1986	1996
View on fertility									
Too high	55	67	86	47	52	59	79	81	59
Satisfactory	52	50	50	45	38	34	16	14	39
Too low	9	13	9	8	10	6	2	2	1
Total	116	130	145	100	100	100	97	97	99
Policy on fertility									
Lower	40	54	81	34	42	56	77	78	85
Maintain	12	10	15	10	8	10	2	2	2
No intervention	58	55	38	50	42	26	17	16	11
Raise	6	11	11	5	8	8	1	1	2
Total	116	130	145	100	100	100	97	97	99
Support for family planning									
Direct support	74	98	115	64	75	79	87	91	95
Indirect support	11	14	11	9	11	8	5	4	2
Limits	7	4	1	6	3	1	2	1	0
No support	24	14	14	21	11	10	3	2	2
No data			4			3			0
Total	116	130	145	100	100	100	97	97	99

Policy Data: https://www.un.org/development/desa/pd/content/older-revisions
Definitions of Policy Variables: https://esa.un.org/poppolicy/img/Definitions_Policy_Variables.pdf
Population Data: World Population Prospects 2019, POP/DB/WPP/Rev.2019/POP/F01-1

from colonialism, and were optimistic that independence would allow economic development to speed forward. Many government leaders came into power with a traditional "mercantilist" perception of population size: larger populations meant greater national strength and wealth potential (Watkins & Hodgson, 2019: 231–234). Many also were saddled with national borders that had been set by colonial powers, and often encompassed a variety of ethnic groups with different languages, customs, and religions. In a democratic context, ethnic competition for political power often inspired a numbers competition that led ethnic groups to favor larger rather than smaller families. Additionally, many African countries had relatively low population densities, and their governments did not fear immediate land or food shortages. The relatively high percentage of Africa's population that lived in a country that "directly supported" family planning (69%) likely reflects the easy availability of international funds for starting family planning programs by that date.

In Africa's case, the twenty years from 1976 to 1996 produced dramatic increases in all three measures indicative of acceptance of a Path 2 approach to fertility transitions. By 1996 87% of Africa's population lived in a country that viewed its fertility

Table 5.2 UN world population policy survey 1976, 1986, 1996: African countries

	# of African countries			Percent of African countries			Percent of population in Africa		
	1976	1986	1996	1976	1986	1996	1976	1986	1996
View on fertility									
Too high	18	31	41	38	61	77	35	76	87
Satisfactory	25	17	11	52	33	21	58	23	13
Too low	5	3	1	10	6	2	3	1	0
Total	48	51	53	100	100	100	97	99	100
Policy on fertility									
Lower	12	21	36	25	41	68	30	55	84
Maintain	2	3	3	4	6	6	1	2	1
No intervention	32	24	12	67	47	23	61	40	13
Raise	2	3	2	4	6	4	4	2	2
Total	48	51	53	100	100	100	96	97	100
Support for family planning									
Direct support	24	38	43	50	75	81	69	85	92
Indirect support	7	6	5	15	12	9	13	10	7
Limits	3	0	0	6	0		2	0	
No support	14	7	4	29	14	8	11	4	1
No data			1			2			0
Total	48	51	53	100	100	100	96	99	100

level as "too high," 84% in a country with a policy to lower fertility, and 92% in a country that gave direct support for family planning. This was the time when most African countries entered into their fertility transitions (Fig. 2.2), and many African couples began experiencing the increase in unwanted and mistimed pregnancies that accompanies a decline in their desired family size (Fig. 3.9).

5.3.2 Questions of Coercion, Reproductive Health and Reproductive Rights

From 1970 to 2000 the international population movement came closer to realizing its goals: more countries adopted policies to lower fertility, and more countries began to experience significant declines in fertility. The movement's success was accompanied by rising concerns over coercion. At the country level, concern arose around issues of sovereignty, the right of each country to independently determine its own national policies and programs. From its beginning, the movement had clear demographic objectives, with the Rockefeller Foundation actually specifying "population

5.3 Controversies During the Rapid Decline Phase, 1970–2000

stabilization" as its goal. Funding education efforts and voluntary family planning programs were its preferred means of attaining "buy-in" by developing countries, but from early on movement advocacy occasionally incited more coercive intrusions. We have seen that President Johnson used the threat of withholding food aid from India to pressure it to "enhance" its family planning program. The World Bank under the presidency of Robert McNamara (1968–1981) made it clear that development money was contingent on establishing family planning programs. The Bank even felt free to specify a country's program specifics. When it thought that the Ministry of Health was doing a poor job running Kenya's family planning program, it made establishing a new National Council on Population and Development "a condition for release of the second tranche of the Second Structural Adjustment Loan" (World Bank, 1992: 54). In 1984 the Reagan administration blocked US family planning assistance to any NGO that provided abortion counselling or referrals, or that advocated for the decriminalization or expansion of abortion services. Because the US played a central role in funding international family planning activities, this coercive "global gag rule" altered the provision of family planning services, significantly depressing their delivery especially in sub-Saharan Africa (Meulen Rodgers, 2018: 13–38).

Where governments independently viewed fertility control as being in their national interest, issues arose over the level of pressure states used to induce individuals to have fewer births. The blatant coercion of China's one-child program garnered world-wide approbation, as did India's forced sterilization campaign. But there was no universal agreement about when the line was crossed in terms of the use of incentives and disincentives. Some thought (Sinding, 2007: 8) that the size of Bangladesh's reimbursement payments for sterilizations and the amount of pressure the Indonesian government put on local leaders to meet contraception targets were coercive. Others, often holding a more dire assessment of these countries' situations, found them not coercive. By the 1980s, though, the very success that many developing countries had with both lowering fertility and expanding their economies began affecting people's judgments about what was acceptable. The reception given the World Bank's *World Development Report 1984*, a sophisticated treatment of "population and development" from a movement perspective, illustrated this point. Richard Easterlin in his review called it a "brief for the World Bank's official position" (Easterlin, 1985: 115) that placed an incorrectly high priority on the need for family planning programs in poor countries and thus inappropriately legitimized coercive "beyond family planning" measures (119).

The 1984 UN Conference on Population in Mexico City marked a turning point in movement development. The Reagan appointed US delegation asserted that "population is a neutral phenomenon" in the development process, and that excessive state control of the economy was more responsible for economic stagnation than rapid population growth. Adopting this anti-Malthusian position undercut the economic development rationale for fertility control programs, and allowed the Reagan administration to oppose the use of any pressure in family planning programs and all induced abortion. Although inspired by domestic political considerations, this position had concrete consequences. In response to the administration's positions, the head of

USAID protected its funding and bureaucracy not only by isolating its family planning programs from all connection with abortion services, but also by elaborating new non-population control rationales, designating them as components of maternal and child health programs (McPherson, 1985). Reproductive rights feminists objected strenuously to USAID's abortion position, but actively endorsed the recasting of family planning as a health program (Dixon-Mueller, 1987).

The question of state attempts to coercively influence women's reproductive decisions has a long history, and opposition to it goes back to the rise of the birth control movement in the early twentieth century. In many developed countries the fertility transition occurred gradually over the course of many decades with the small family norm being adopted first by the upper classes. At the time a number of governments passed laws that criminalized both contraception and abortion. Movements arose in both the US and Great Britain with the goal of legalizing contraception. In 1952 eight of these national family planning associations met in Bombay, India and established the International Planned Parenthood Association with Margret Sanger as its president. She imprinted it with her feminist belief that birth control was essential for women's equality. She believed that all women desired to control their fertility but simply lacked the means to do so. IPPF representatives and members of the Population Council met in 1955, 1956, and 1957 "to develop and define general principles for promoting birth control overseas" (Piotrow, 1973: 14).

But second-wave feminism, which arose in the 1960s, aligned more with the civil rights and anti-war movements than with the early birth control movement (Hodgson & Watkins, 1997). Some radical feminists began questioning the motives behind First World interest in controlling Third World women's fertility. The term "reproductive rights" entered the feminist lexicon during the decade 1975–1985. Originally it was a counterpoint offered by leftist feminists to the focus on "abortion rights" by liberal feminists. It aimed at broadening the feminist reproductive agenda: women should have more than just a right to an abortion, they should have full "reproductive rights" to a government-subsidized abortion in case of need, contraception, prenatal care, and early childhood health care. And all women, including poor women, should have the right to have as many children as they wanted.

Beginning in the mid-1980s, a network of feminists committed to improving women's reproductive health "played an increasingly influential role both in shaping the terms of the policy debate and re-orienting the population agendas of major international institutions" (Higer, 1997: 1). The Cold War fears that had generated a good deal of political support for population control efforts for 40 years had ended with the collapse of the Soviet Union. Family planning programs continued to receive international funding, but an increasing proportion of funding was provided by governments of developing countries themselves, indicating a growing commitment to family planning on their part. By 1996 the developing world had about 95% of its population living in countries that "directly supported" family planning activities (Table 5.1), its total fertility rate had fallen to about 3 (Fig. 1.1), and a significant number of countries had completed their fertility transitions (Fig. 2.4). This success took some of the urgency from the fertility control movement, and its advocates began seeking new allies. The environmental movement seemed an obvious candidate, given that one strand of explanation for environmental problems emphasized population growth. But women meeting in Rio de Janeiro in preparation for the 1992 UN Conference on Environment and Development objected vigorously and successfully to including population as a cause of environmental degradation. They feared that blaming environmental degradation on the prolificness of the poor rather than on the overconsumption of the rich would simply provide a rationale for restricting the reproductive rights of women in developing countries.

At the 1994 International Conference on Population and Development in Cairo the new alliance that came to sustain the movement was largely initiated by feminists. Its Program of Action (United Nations, 1994) assigned in Principle 4 an explicit feminist agenda to population programs: "Advancing gender equality and equity and the empowerment of women, and the elimination of all kinds of violence against women, and ensuring women's ability to control their own fertility, are cornerstones of population and development-related programmes." It offered a rationale for this partiality by asserting (3.16) that "eliminating social, cultural, political and economic discrimination against women" is a "prerequisite" for "achieving balance between population and available resources." Protecting the individual rights of women was presented as an indispensable means for achieving neo-Malthusian ends. Although many had expected Cairo would be a battleground where feminists and neo-Malthusians would fight over framing the world's population agenda, there was little hostility between the two. They actually became allies in the one controversy that did erupt at Cairo. They fought, largely unsuccessfully, against a Vatican delegation intent on keeping any mention of abortion out of the Program of Action. Great care was taken at Cairo to define "family planning" and "birth control" in ways that explicitly excluded abortion, as had been the case in all previous UN Programs of Action.

5.3.3 *Does Fertility Decline Promote Development? Do Family Planning Programs Promote Fertility Decline?*

As evidence of substantial fertility decline became clearer, the level of controversy over fertility policy declined in the international arena. The Green Revolution allayed the fears of mass famine that arose in the 1960s by increasing crop yields in the developing world by 75% from 1962 to 1989 (Bongaarts, 1996: 488–489). This increase alone was almost enough to feed the concurrent 84% increase in the developing world's population. Preston (1987: 628–634) explained the fall-off in "alarmist" international discussion by pointing to the developing world's rapid rates of per capita economic growth (especially high in countries with market economies) and its declining fertility. While these trends lessened international worries, they provoked greater controversy in academic circles. This controversy revolved around whether two foundational premises of the neo-Malthusian movement were true: fertility decline will promote economic development; family planning programs will promote fertility decline.

At mid-century the agreement about the severity of the population crisis among most demographers had smoothed over tensions arising from the contradictory demands of objectivity and advocacy (Hodgson, 1983). Demographic transition specialists were able to overlook the policy implication of their original theory and became advocates of an international population control movement even in the absence of much evidence supporting its feasibility. But as the population crisis receded, it became more difficult for some demographers to incorporate the optimistic economic and demographic trends of the 1970 and 1980s into their discipline. The near-zero correlation during these decades between population growth and per capita economic growth within the developing world led Preston (1987: 628) to conclude "population growth could not be an overriding factor in economic growth." This near zero correlation had been noted 20 years earlier by Kuznets (1967: 190–191) and Easterlin (1967), but then it could be ignored as a temporal anomaly due to the sparsity of significant fertility decline. But as the developing world's fertility transition accelerated, some, most notably (Simon, 1981), were so emboldened by this lack of association as to present true movement heresy: population growth stimulates economic growth.

Increasingly sceptics were given a serious hearing, especially after the National Research Council published in 1986 *Population Growth and Economic Development: Policy Questions*. It noted (National Research Council, 1986) on its first page the developing world's falling total fertility rate (from 6.2 in 1950–1955 to 4.1 in 1980–1985) and on page 5 the positive annual growth rates of real gross domestic product per capita (ranging from 2.4% to 3.5% for the entire developing world over the period 1950–1960 to 1965–1970 and approximating 5.5% in the East Asia and Pacific region over the period 1965–1981). The pessimism endemic to works relating population growth and development from the time of Coale and Hoover's (1958) study was laid open to doubt: "But it is clear that despite rapid population growth, developing countries have achieved unprecedented levels of income per capita, literacy, and life expectancy over the past 25 years."

More than thirty years has passed since the publication of the National Research Council's study. Many additional developing countries have completed their fertility transitions and the developing world's rate of population growth has declined by a full percentage point, from an annual rate of 2.2% in 1986 to 1.2% in 2020. The demographic effects of fertility decline on age structure also have become more evident, and the effects of these changes on the economy have been the focus of considerable study. In Chap. 6 we will examine in more detail what is currently known about the relationship between fertility decline and economic development and demonstrate that this relationship is more complex than suggested by NRC report. In particular new evidence indicates that fertility decline stimulates growth in income per capita.

Do family planning programs promote fertility decline? In a 1994 article Lant Pritchett, using data from World Fertility Surveys and Demographic and Health Surveys from the 1970s and 1980s, questioned whether family planning programs had much effect on rates of fertility decline. He found (Pritchett, 1994) that "ninety percent of the differences across countries in total fertility rates are accounted for solely by differences in women's reported desired fertility," and that "in spite of the obvious role of contraception as a proximate determinant of fertility, the additional effect of contraceptive availability or family planning programs on fertility is quantitatively small and explains very little cross-country variation." Now there is more than thirty years of additional data to use when examining this question. Many more developing countries, with more varied backgrounds, have entered the middle and late phases of their fertility transitions. In Chap. 7 we will examine what is currently known about the extent to which family planning programs promote fertility decline and document the shortcomings in the Pritchett study. Unravelling these relationships is central to better understanding how the developing world's fertility transition occurred, and what it might mean for the welfare of its population.

5.3.4 Africa and the AIDS Crisis

As the twentieth century ended, most women in developing countries were actively controlling their fertility, their children were attending schools for longer periods, and extreme poverty was less common. The heated mid-century controversies over the population crisis had died down considerably. Areas of Africa were the exception. In Middle, West, and East Africa women were still giving birth to over six children (Fig. 1.3), some countries were seeing their fertility transitions stall (Fig. 2.5), and fewer than 20% of couples were using contraception (Fig. 3.6). The mid-century population crisis seemed to have assumed a narrower geographic focus. But mortality conditions in Africa were very different than those present at mid-century. Instead of life expectancy increasing significantly, from 1985 to 2000 sub-Saharan Africa experienced no improvement at all, with many countries suffering dramatic declines: Zimbabwe life expectancy went from 61 to 45, in Botswana it went from 61 to 51, in Kenya from 59 to 51, in the Central African Republic from 50 to 44, and in South Africa from 61 to 55.

AIDS was initially recognized in Africa in 1983, although the true magnitude of the epidermic took time to come into focus (Quinn 2001: 1156–1157). In 1986 WHO estimated the annual number of new AIDS cases in Africa at 400,000 with between 1 to 2 million Africans being HIV-infected. By 2000 the reality was very different: an estimated 25.3 million Africans HIV-infected with 3.8 million new cases being reported that year. Sixteen countries had more that 10% of their adult population aged 15–49 HIV-infected. In the 1990s demographers and epidemiologists incorporated the severity of the AIDS epidemic into their projections of African population growth. Anderson et al. (1991: 558) concluded that the only uncertainty was "whether AIDS induced mortality will decrease population size over a few or many decades." Gregson et al. (1994: 843) produced two simulations of sub-Saharan Africa's population growth, one with the annual population growth rate by the fifteenth year of the epidemic falling from 2.6% to less than 1%, and the other with it falling into negative territory (−0.9%). The 2000 Revision of the UN's World Population Prospects (United Nations Population Division, 2001: 13) estimated that the thirty-five most affected African countries experienced 8.3 million additional deaths due to AIDS from 1995 to 2000, projected that by 2010–2015 excess deaths would reach 14.5 million and that South Africa would have negative population growth.

5.4 Conclusion

The population crisis that loomed so large at mid-century nearly disappeared from international discourse as the year 2000 approached. The one region which still had significant ground to cover in its fertility transition faced an AIDS epidemic that rolled back decades' worth of mortality improvements, devastated innumerable families, and promised to balance birth and death rates in a most disastrous fashion. At the time no one knew how the AIDS crisis would end. Scientists, policy makers, leaders of NGOs, and international organizations all placed AIDS high on their agendas, and funds flowed into AIDS research and prevention efforts. Meanwhile the US was reducing its funding for bilateral international family planning (DaVanzo & Adamson, 1998). World leaders met at the Millennium Summit held at the UN headquarters in New York City in September of 2000 and promulgated the United Nations Millennium Declaration (2000) that set the international policy agenda for the first decades of the twenty-first century. It included sections on peace and disarmament, development and poverty eradication, protecting the environment, meeting the special needs of Africa, and strengthening the United Nations. There was no mention of "population," "family planning," or "fertility" in the document. The Declaration served as the basis for the later elaboration of the eight Millennium Development Goals and the specification of twenty-one specific targets that all countries should try to meet by 2015. Only one of the twenty-one targets (5B)—"achieve, by 2015, universal access to reproductive health"—bore any connection to family planning.

The century ended with the average women living in the developing world giving birth to just 2.9 children (Fig. 1.1), indicating a successfully traversing of the fertility transition. While this was true for the developing world in the aggregate, it was not true for much of Africa (Fig. 1.3), where fertility levels in 2000 looked much like they did in 1950. These areas faced exceptional challenges with respect to successfully completing their fertility transitions: an ongoing AIDS epidemic, and an international community which no longer had lowering high fertility as a central policy goal.

References

Ahlberg, K. (2007). Machiavelli with a heart: The Johnson administration's food for peace program in India, 1965–1966. *Diplomatic History, 31*(4), 665–701.

Anderson, R., et al. (1991). The spread of HIV-1 in Africa: Sexual contact patterns and the predicted demographic impact of AIDS. *Nature, 352*, 581–589.

References

Bongaarts, J. (1996). Population pressure and the food supply system in the developing world. *Population and Development Review, 22*(3), 483–503.

Bonner, J. (1967). Review: A challenge to those who would avert starvation. *Science, 157*(3791), 914–915.

Borlaug, N. (1970). *Acceptance speech for noble prize for peace*. https://www.nobelprize.org/prizes/peace/1970/borlaug/lecture/.

Caldwell, J. (2002). Thirty years of global population changes. In N. Sadik (Ed.), *An agenda for people: UNFPA through three decades* (pp. 2–23). NYU Press.

Caldwell, J., & Caldwell, P. (1986). *Limiting population growth and the Ford Foundation contribution*. Frances Pinter.

Coale, A. (1969). The decline of fertility in Europe from the French Revolution to World War II. In S. Behrman (Ed.), *Fertility and family planning: A world view* (pp. 3–24). University of Michigan Press.

Coale, A., & Hoover, E. (1958). *Population growth and economic development in low-income countries*. Princeton University Press.

Commission on population growth and the American future. (1972). *Population and the American future*. Superintendent of Documents.

Connelly, M. (2008). *Fatal misconception: The struggle to control world population*. Harvard University Press.

DaVanzo, J., & Adamson, D. (1998). Family planning in developing countries: An unfinished success story. RAND Corporation. https://www.rand.org/pubs/issue_papers/IP176.html.

Davis, K. (1945). The world demographic transition. *Annals of the American Academy of Political and Social Science, 237*, 1–11.

Davis, K. (1946). Human fertility in India. *American Journal of Sociology, 52*(3), 243–254.

Davis, K. (1950a). Population and change in backward areas. *Columbia Journal of International Affairs, 4*(2), 41–51.

Davis, K. (1950b). Population and the further spread of industrial society. *Proceedings of the American Philosophical Society 95*,(1), 8–19.

Davis, K. (1953). Future population trends and their significance. *Transactions of the eighteenth North American wildlife conference* (pp. 8–21). Wildlife Management Institute.

Davis, K. (1954). Fertility control and the demographic transition in India. In *The interrelations of demographic, economic, and social problems in selected underdeveloped areas*. Milbank Memorial Fund.

Davis, K. (1956). Population and power in the free world. In T. Free, J. Spengler & O. Duncan (Eds.), *Population theory and policy* (pp. 342–356). Press.

Davis, K. (1967). Population policy: Will current programs succeed? *Science, 158*, 730–739.

Dixon-Mueller, R. (1987). U.S. international population policy and "The Woman Question." *Journal of International Law and Politics 20*(1), 143–167.

Easterlin, R. (1967). Effects of population growth on the economic development of developing countries. *Annals of the American Academy of Political and Social Science, 369*, 98–108.

Easterlin, R. (1985). Review of world development report 1984—world bank. *Population and Development Review, 11*(1), 113–119.

Ehrlich, P. (1968). *The population bomb*. Ballantine.

Fawcett, J. (1970). *Psychology and population*. The Population Council.

Finkle, J., & Crane, B. (1975). The politics of Bucharest: Population, development, and the new international economic order. *Population and Development Review, 1*(1), 87–114.

Ford Foundation. (1985). *The Ford foundation's work in population* (Ford Foundation Working Paper).

Gregson, S., Garnett, G., & Anderson, R. (1994). Is HIV-1 likely to become a leading cause of adult mortality in sub-Saharan Africa? *Journal of Acquired Immune Deficiency Syndromes, 7*, 839–852.

Hardin, G. (1968). The tragedy of the commons. *Science, 162*, 1243–1248.

Harkavy, O. (1995). *Curbing population growth: An insider's perspective on the population movement*. Plenum Press.
Hauser, P. (1960). Demographic dimensions of world politics. *Science, 131*(3414), 1641–1647.
Hauser, P. (1967). Family planning and population programs: A book review article. *Demography, 4*(1), 397–414.
Higer, A. (1997). Transnational movements and world politics: The international women's health movement and population policy. Unpublished Ph.D. dissertation, Brandeis University.
Hodgson, D. (1983). Demography as social science and policy science. *Population and Development Review, 9*(1), 1–34.
Hodgson, D. (1988). Orthodoxy and revisionism in American demography. *Population and Development Review, 14*(4), 541–569.
Hodgson, D., & Watkins, S. (1997). Feminists and neo-Malthusians: Past and present alliances. *Population and Development Review, 23*(3), 469–523.
Hyrenius, H., & Åhs, U. (1968). Ceylon: The Sweden-Ceylon family planning pilot project. *Studies in Family Planning, 1*(36), 6–11.
Johnson, L. (1965a). *State of the union message*. https://www.presidency.ucsb.edu/documents/annual-message-the-congress-the-state-the-union-26..
Johnson, L. (1965b). *Address in San Francisco at the 20th anniversary commemorative session of the United Nations*. https://www.presidency.ucsb.edu/node/241692.
Johnson, L. (1966). President Johnson's message to Congress on foreign assistance. *The State Department Bulletin 54*, 1392
Kirk, D. (1944). Population changes and the postwar world. *American Sociological Review, 9*(1), 28–35.
Kuznets, S. (1967). Population and economic growth. *Proceedings of the American Philosophical Society, 111*(3), 170–193.
Leibenstein, H. (1954). *A Theory of economic-demographic development*. Princeton University Press.
McPherson, P. (1985). *International family planning: The reasons for the program*. Speech delivered to the American Enterprise Institute.
Meulen Rodgers, Y. (2018). *The global gag rule and women's reproductive health: Rhetoric versus reality*. Oxford University Press.
Myrdal, G. (1970). *The challenge of world poverty: A world anti-poverty program in outline*. Pantheon Books.
National Research Council. (1986). *Population growth and economic development: Policy questions*. National Academy Press.
Nelson, R. (1956). A theory of the low-level equilibrium trap in underdeveloped countries. *American Economic Review, 46*(5), 894–908.
Notestein, F. (1945). Population-the long view. In T. Schultz (Ed.), *Food for the world* (pp. 36–57). University of Chicago Press.
Notestein, F. (1953). Economic problems of population change. In *Proceedings of the Eighth International Conference of Agricultural Economists* (pp. 13–31). University Press.
Notestein, F. (1971). Reminiscences: The role of foundations, of the Population Association of America, Princeton University and the United Nations in fostering American interest in population problems. *Milbank Memorial Fund Quarterly, 49*(4), 67–85.
Paddock, W., & Paddock, P. (1967). *Famine—1975! America's decision: Who will survive?* Little Brown.
Paterson, A. (1947). The pax britannica and the population; the human situation in East Africa—Part I: On the increase of people; Part II: Towards a population policy. *East African Medical Journal 24*, 77–80, 81–97, 144–151.
Piotrow, P. (1973). *World population crisis: The United States response*. Praeger.
Preston, S. (1987). The social sciences and the population problem. *Sociological Forum, 2*(4), 619–644.

References

Pritchett, L. (1994). Desired fertility and the impact of population policies. *Population and Development Review, 20*(1), 1–55.

Quinn, T. (2001). AIDS in Africa: A retrospective. *Bulletin of the World Health Organization, 79*(12), 1156–1158.

Rockefeller, J. (1974). Population growth: The role of the developed world. In *Lecture series on population. International union for the scientific study of population.* Liege. Reprinted in full in *Population and Development Review 4*(3), 509–516.

Simon, J. (1981). *The ultimate resource.* Princeton University Press.

Sinding, S. (2007). Overview and perspective. In W. Robinson & J. Ross (Eds.), *The global family planning revolution: Three decades of population policies and programs* (pp. 1–12). The World Bank.

Thompson, W. (1946). *Population and peace in the pacific.* University of Chicago Press.

United Nation. (1994). Program of action. In *Adopted at the international conference on population and development.* Cairo. https://www.unfpa.org/sites/default/files/event-pdf/PoA_en.pdf.

United Nations. (2000). United Nations millennium declaration. General Assembly, 18 September 2000, A/RES/55/2. https://www.un.org/en/development/desa/population/migration/generalassembly/docs/globalcompact/A_RES_55_2.pdf.

United Nations Population Division. (2001). World population prospects 2000: Highlights, online: http://enerpedia.net/images/2/2c/Wpp2000h.pdf.

United Nations Population Division. (2019). World population prospects 2019, Online Edition. Rev.1. Department of Economic and Social Affairs, United Nations (File INT/1: Interpolated demographic indicators by region, subregion and country, annually for 1950–2099).

Warwick, D. (1982). *Bitter pills: Population policies and their implementation in eight developing countries.* Cambridge University Press.

Watkins, S., & Hodgson, D. (2019). Developmental idealism, the international population movement, and the transformation of population ideology in Kenya. *Sociology of Development, 5*(3), 229–247.

Westoff, C., & McCarthy, J. (1979). Population attitudes and fertility. *Family Planning Perspectives, 11*(2), 93–96.

World Bank. (1992). Kenya. *Operations evaluation department, population and the world bank: Implications from eight case studies* (pp. 50–55).

Open Access This chapter is licensed under the terms of the Creative Commons Attribution 4.0 International License (http://creativecommons.org/licenses/by/4.0/), which permits use, sharing, adaptation, distribution and reproduction in any medium or format, as long as you give appropriate credit to the original author(s) and the source, provide a link to the Creative Commons license and indicate if changes were made.

The images or other third party material in this chapter are included in the chapter's Creative Commons license, unless indicated otherwise in a credit line to the material. If material is not included in the chapter's Creative Commons license and your intended use is not permitted by statutory regulation or exceeds the permitted use, you will need to obtain permission directly from the copyright holder.

Chapter 6
Does Fertility Decline Stimulate Development?

6.1 Introduction

Economists have debated the potential impact of demographic change on economic growth since Malthus. The consensus on this relationship has shifted repeatedly since the late 1950s when Coale and Hoover (1958) published their influential study. They argued that rapid population growth inhibits growth in per capita income because the savings needed to raise human and physical capital per capita are higher in rapidly than in slowly growing populations. Population growth absorbs savings that could be used to increase capital intensity and raise per capita output. Coale and Hoover also concluded that rapid population growth and high fertility lead to a high proportion of children in the population, which limits savings needed for growing economies. Ministers of finance and development planning experts throughout the developing world realized that rapid population growth would require large investments in education, health services, housing, agriculture, and infrastructure just to keep up with population growth, thus leaving few resources to increase standards of living. From the 1950s to the mid-1970s, concerns about the adverse economic and environmental effects of rapid population growth dominated academic, political, and popular thinking (NAS, 1971)

This consensus came to an end when empirical studies from the late 1960 and 1970s failed to confirm an inverse correlation between the population growth rate and the growth rate of per capita output of countries (Headey & Hodge, 2009, 2001; Kuznets, 1967). This finding contradicted expectations arising from Coale and Hoover' analysis and led to a revisionist view that population growth is largely a neutral or even a positive factor in development (Simon, 1981).

This revisionist view itself was overturned during the 1990s as more sophisticated models were developed and data from the 1980 and 1990s became available. The previously insignificant correlation between population growth and growth of per capita output turned negative (Headey & Hodge, 2009; Kelley & Schmidt, 1995, 2001). A plausible explanation for these initially puzzling findings was provided in a thorough review of the evidence by Kelley and Schmidt (1995, 2001). They concluded that declines in mortality, fertility, and population growth all have positive effects on economic growth per capita. These findings helped explain the change over time in the correlation between population and economic growth. For example, the studies using pre-1980 data often included many developing countries that were experiencing rapid mortality decline as well as accelerating population growth. According to Kelley and Schmidt's findings, the former's positive effect on economic growth was offset by the latter's negative effect, thus producing an unexpected absence of a correlation. In subsequent decades, mortality decline slowed, fertility declined rapidly, and population growth slowed. The negative correlation between growth and development observed from the 1980s onward could be explained by the combined effects of declines in fertility and declining growth rates, both of which enhance economic growth.

A further important development occurred in the 1990s when seminal research by Barro (1991, 1997) identified fertility decline as an important factor in economic growth. The finding was of great interest to policymakers and led to a set of new studies by economists of what is now called the "demographic dividend." This dividend offers a potential boost to GDP per capita when fertility decline leads to a rise in the ratio of workers to dependents. The period during which the dividend is available is bounded but can range up to decades.

This chapter reviews the evidence for the demographic dividend in the developing world. We first summarize the magnitude and timing of the age-structure changes caused by fertility decline. This is followed by a discussion of the first and second demographic dividends provided by these changes in the age-structure. We conclude with a summary of a range of multi-sectoral non-economic benefits of fertility decline.

6.2 Age Structure Effects of Declining Fertility

Before the onset of the fertility transition, populations typically have an age pyramid that is wide at the bottom (many young people) and narrow at the top (few old people). Figure 6.1 plots the age structures of the population of the developing world in 1970 and 2020. The 1970 population had the young age structure typical of pre-transitional populations with half of the population under age 18. The fertility decline after 1970 has shrunk the under 18 population to just 32% of the total population in 2020. As expected, this decline is accompanied by an equivalent increase in the population above age 18. The population of working age (18–64) rose from 48 to 60% between 1970 and 2020, and the 65+ population rose from 4 to 7%. These changes in the population age structure, which are largely the result of declining fertility, are the first of the demographic dividends.

Figures 6.2 and 6.3 examine trends in measures of the age structure by region (estimates to 2020, projections to 2100). About half of the population was under age 18 before 1970 in Asia, Latin America, and SSA (see Fig. 6.2). During the 1950

6.2 Age Structure Effects of Declining Fertility

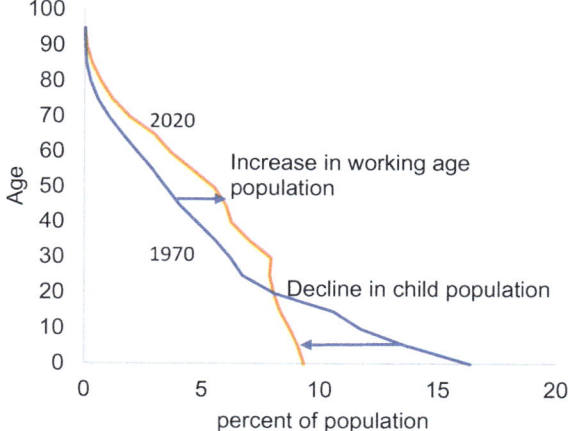

Fig. 6.1 Population distribution by age of the developing world, 1970 and 2020 (UN Population Division, 2019)

and 1960s the proportion under age 18 actually rose slightly as a result of a decline in child mortality. However, as fertility declines proceeded in Latin America and Asia/N.Africa in the 1970 and 1980s, the proportion of children declined rapidly to around 30% by 2020 (United Nations Population Division, 2019). In contrast, the decline in the child population in SSA started later—around 2000—and was slower as a result of later and slower fertility declines. As expected, there is a close correspondence between trends in fertility and trends in the proportion under 18, although the latter follows the former with a delay of one to two decades (compare Figs. 2.1 and 6.2). Projections to 2100 indicate further declines in the proportion under 18 dropping below 20% in Asia/N. Africa and L. America. This downward trend is largely due to a continuing rise in the population over 65.

Another important indicator of the changing age structure is the proportion of the population of working age (usually taken to be between 18 and 64 years), which is often referred to as the "support ratio". Figure 6.3 plots estimates and projections of regional averages of this proportion from 1950 to 2100. In Asia/N.Africa and Latin America, the substantial declines in the proportion under age 18 after 1970 led to a sharp rise in the proportion aged 18–64 between 1970 and about 2020. In future

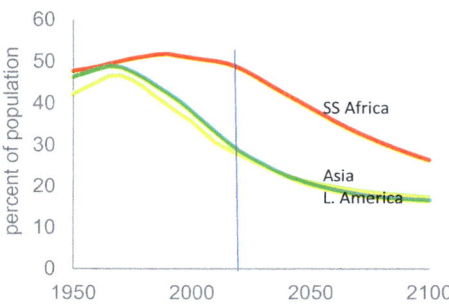

Fig. 6.2 Percent of population under age 18, 1950–2100 (UN Population Division, 2019)

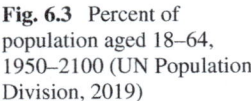

Fig. 6.3 Percent of population aged 18–64, 1950–2100 (UN Population Division, 2019)

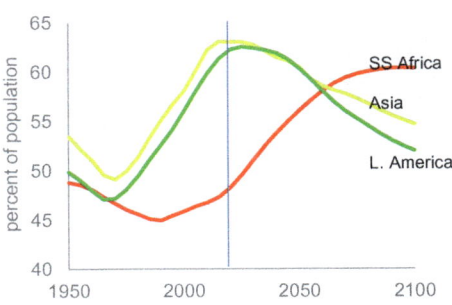

decades this proportion declines again as earlier fertility reductions eventually lead to a smaller working age proportion and a larger 65+ proportion. A quite different pattern is evident in SSA, where the later and slower onset of the fertility decline leads to a delayed rise in the proportion of working age relative to other regions.

6.3 The Components of Growth in GDP Per Capita

A brief discussion of basic economic arithmetic is useful to understand how changes in the population age-structure affect economic growth. Analyses of the growth of national economies often rely on a decomposition of GDP per capita and its growth rate into three largely independent factors (World Bank, 2016):

(1) *Support ratio*, defined as the proportion of the total population that is of working-age.
(2) *Labor force participation rate*, defined as the proportion of the working-age population (18–64) that is employed.
(3) *Productivity*, defined as the GDP per worker.

In any given year the *level* of the GDP per capita of a population equals the *product* of these three factors. In addition, the *growth rate* in the GDP per capita in that year equals the *sum* of (1) rate of change in the support ratio; (2) the rate of change in labor force participation rate; and (3) the rate of change in productivity. These equations indicate that, everything else constant, a 1% increase per year of the support ratio (or any one of the other two factors) results in an equivalent 1% increase in GDP per capita. If all three factors increase by 1% per year, GDP per capita rises at 3% per year.

6.4 The First Demographic Dividend

The first demographic dividend (also called the arithmetic dividend or the labor-force accelerating effect) refers to the rise in GDP per capita that results, other things being equal, from an increase in the support ratio as the population age-structure changes over time. (Ahmed & Cruz, 2016; Bloom & Williamson, 1998; Bloom & Canning, 2004; Bloom et al., 2009; Canning et al., 2015; Cruz & Ahmed, 2016; Eastwood & Lipton, 2011; Higgins & Williamson, 1997; Kelley & Schmidt, 1995, 2005, 2007; Karra, Canning, & Wilde, 2017; Lee & Mason, 2006; Mason & Kinugasa, 2008; World Bank, 2015). This dividend is independent of any changes or improvements in productivity or the labor force participation rate.

The second demographic dividend refers to additional increases in per capita income that result from changes in productivity or the labor force participation rate as the age structure changes and savings rise; it will be discussed in the next section.

Figure 6.4 plots the first dividends for each region expressed in percent per year change. These plots are directly derived from the support ratios plotted in Fig. 6.3. The first dividend (i.e., the growth rate in the support ratio) is *positive* when the support ratio is *rising* and *negative* when the support ratio is *declining*. For example, in Latin America the support ratio rose from 47 to 62% between 1967 and 2024; these are the years during which the dividend is positive. In the years before 1967 and after 2024 the dividend is negative. Over the period from 1950 to 2100 the dividend starts negative (as declines in child mortality raise the youth population) and ends negative (as the share of the population over 65 increases quickly). In the intervening years the dividend is positive and the economic growth per capita receives a boost.

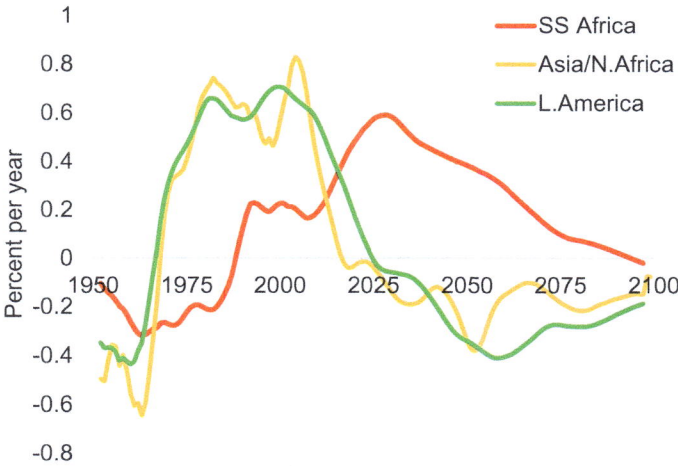

Fig. 6.4 First dividend by region 1950–2100 (Authors' calculations from UN Population Division, 2019)

Table 6.1 Selected statistics on the positive first dividend by region

	Timing of first dividend			Magnitude of first dividend (percent/year)		
	Start	End	Duration	Peak	Average	Cumulative
SS Africa	1989	2093	104	0.59	0.28	34.4
Asia/N.Africa	1968	2016	48	0.83	0.51	28.4
L.America	1967	2024	57	0.71	0.49	33.0

Source Mason et al. (2017)

The timing of the (positive) dividend years varies widely among countries and regions. As shown in Fig. 6.4 and Table 6.1 the dividend patterns are broadly similar for Asia/N.Africa and Latin America. In these regions the dividend onset was in the late 1960s and lasted about half a century. Peak dividends reach around 0.7–0.8% per year. In the future the economies of these regions face headwinds from the slightly negative first dividends. It should be emphasized that the estimates in Table 6.1 are regional averages and the peak values for individual countries can be substantially higher. For example, in several East Asian countries the first dividend peaked at over 2%. This means that the growth rate in GDP per capita in these countries were raised by 2% from the first dividend.

In sub-Saharan Africa the positive first dividend period starts later (in 1989) and ends much later—near the end of the twenty-first century. Its average value is about half that of the other region. The net result of the longer but less intense dividend is that SS Africa has a cumulative dividend of 34.4% which is slightly higher than in Asia/N.Africa (28%) and L.America (33%). The first dividend for SS Africa lies still mostly in the future while little dividend is left for the rest of the developing world.

6.5 The Second Demographic Dividend

The second dividend arises when faster growth of the working-age population leads to higher productivity per worker. As the number of dependents declines, workers are able to save more which leads to higher investment in human and physical capital thus raising productivity. Estimates of the second dividend are based on complex statistical models, see, for example, Ashraf et al. (2013), Karra et al. (2017), Mason et al. (2017). The findings of these studies are not easy to compare because the underlying assumptions of the models vary. One of the most comprehensive examinations of the two dividends is provided in a UN Technical Paper by Mason et al. Their main results are summarized in Figs. 6.5 and 6.6.

Figure 6.5 presents estimates of the first, second and total dividend between 1955 and 2015. The dividend is expressed as the cumulative impact on the GDP per capita by the end of the period.

6.5 The Second Demographic Dividend

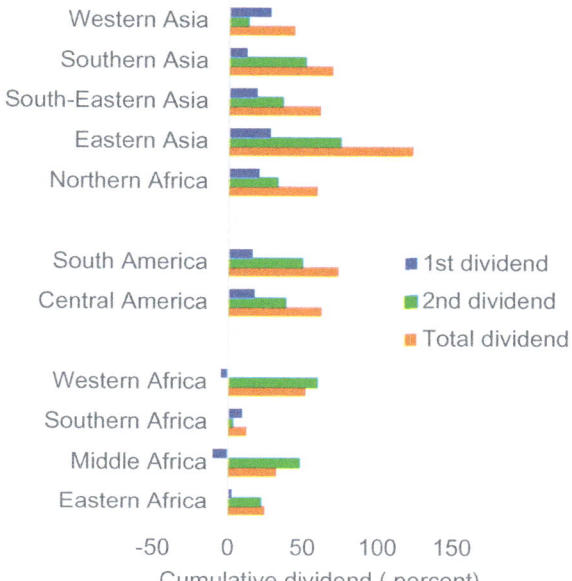

Fig. 6.5 Cumulative first and second dividend 1955–2015 (percent) by region (Mason et al., 2017)

Fig. 6.6 Projected cumulative dividend 2015–2075 (percent) by region (Mason et al., 2017)

As expected from the discussion in the previous section, the cumulative effects of the first dividend are highest in Asia/N.Africa and Latin America and smallest in sub-Saharan Africa. In fact, the dividend is negative in Western and Middle Africa. In these two sub-regions fertility changed little but child mortality dropped rapidly, resulting in a slight increase in the child population.

The cumulative effects of the second dividend for the period 1955–2015 are larger than the first dividend in all regions. As is the case for the first dividend, the second and total dividends are highest in Asia/N.Africa and L. America. In Eastern Asia the cumulative impact of the total dividend reaches 123% which means that the GDP per capita in 2015 was 123% larger than what it would have been without the dividend.

Mason et al. (2017) also look toward the future and project the dividend from 2015 to 2075. This exercise relies on the medium variant of the UN population projections. The results are presented in Fig. 6.6.

In the future the regional differences in cumulative first dividends from 2015 to 2075 are mostly the reverse of what was observed for 1955–2015. That is, the first dividend is negative in Asia/ N. Africa and Latin America, but positive in sub-Saharan Africa. In contrast, the future second dividend is substantial in all regions. It might seem surprising that the first and second dividend can have opposite impact. For example, in East Asia which has substantial negative future first dividend of −22% (because of low fertility in the past and rapid population aging), but it has substantially positive second dividend because of investments in physical and human capital that were made in previous years. As a result, this subregion still has a positive total dividend of 17% between 2015 and 2075.

The regional estimates presented in Figs. 6.5 and 6.6 and in Table 6.1 were all taken from Mason et al. (2017). This study does not contain country specific estimates. However, two recent studies provide comparable country projections of the dividend: one on Democratic Republic of the Congo by Hassan et al. (2019) and another on Nigeria by Mason et al. (2016). These two studies produce a cumulative estimates dividend to 2075 of 88% for Congo DR and 84% for Nigeria.

To summarize, the first dividend yields a mechanical but transitory bonus, that is more-or-less automatic because it depends only on a changing age structure (but assumes no offsetting changes in labor force participation or productivity). The second dividend transforms that bonus into greater productivity and sustainable development. This outcome is not automatic but depends on the implementation of effective policies that encourage savings and productive investments such as in a well-educated labor force. The dividend provides an opportunity for accelerated GDP growth, rather than a guarantee of improved standards of living (Lee & Mason, 2006).

6.6 Multi-sectoral Benefits from Fertility Decline

The preceding sections of this chapter focused on the stimulus to economic growth that countries derive from the demographic dividend. This focus is understandable given the high levels of poverty that still exist in much of the developing world. But the dividend is only one of the many benefits provided by fertility decline and the resulting slower population growth. As women have fewer children, several other development sectors benefit:

Women's empowerment: Women with smaller families have more time and freedom to participate in the formal and informal labor force and civic life;

Health: The reduction in unintended pregnancies and the wider spacing of pregnancies reduce maternal mortality and morbidity and improve infant and child survival and health;

Government: Lower fertility means less pressure on the education and health care sectors and on the country's infrastructure (e.g., transportation, communication, energy, water and sanitation). If population growth continues at a rapid pace, high unemployment rates, explosive growth of slum populations, overcrowded schools and health facilities, and dilapidated public infrastructure will continue to hamper development;

Environment: Reduced pressure on natural resources on which people's lives depend (e.g., fresh water, soil, forest, arable land, energy, etc.) and reduced air, water, and soil pollution; and.

Social/Political stability: With a slower-growing youth population there is less competition for jobs and fewer unemployed youth, thus making political environments more stable.

A fuller examination of the links between the fertility and contraceptive transition and these multi-sectoral effects is beyond the scope of our analysis, but the interested reader can find more detail and extensive references in Starbird et al. (2016). These wide-ranging positive effects of fertility decline make government investments in programs to promote contraceptive use and fertility control more appropriate and consequential.

6.7 Conclusion

In recent decades the literature on the effect of population on development has focused on the demographic dividend. There is now a near consensus—supported by the evidence summarized above—that the dividend is substantial. It is caused by a decline in fertility which leads to a changing age structure with rising numbers of workers and fewer dependents. This increase in the support ratio directly raises the GPD per capita (i.e., the first dividend) and leads to higher savings which allow intensification of human and physical capital (i.e., the second dividend). In general, the second dividend is substantially larger and lasts longer than the first dividend. The first dividend can last many decades, but is ultimately transitory, while the second dividend results in higher productivity and sustainable growth, yielding lasting benefits.

The duration and magnitude of these dividends vary from country to country and depend heavily on the pace and magnitude of the fertility decline. Over the six decades from 1955 to 2015, the first and second dividend together were highest in Asia, N.Africa and Latin America (where the fertility transition was completed quickly and early) and lowest in SS Africa (where the fertility transition was slower and later). Projections for the next six decades to 2075 expect the situation to reverse with the dividend in Asia likely to be smaller than in SS Africa.

Past acceleration in economic growth brought about by the dividend has not been sufficient for a developing country to "vault into the ranks of the developed" (National

Research Council, 1986). But this is obviously an inappropriate expectation. The dividend should be seen as an important stimulus to economic growth during a period when countries are typically still poor. The past dividend has boosted GDP per capita by 50 to more than 100% in most of Asia, N.Africa and Latin America.

The key policy question arising from the now well-established demographic dividends and the multiple other benefits from fertility reduction is whether family planning programs can accelerate fertility decline. This next chapter will take up this still controversial issue.

References

Ahmed, A., & Cruz, M. (2016). *Making the most of demographic change in Southern Africa*. World Bank Policy Research Working Paper 7798. World Bank Group.

Ashraf, Q., Weil, D., & Wilde, J. (2013). The effect of fertility reduction on economic growth. *Population and Development Review, 39*(1), 97–130.

Barro, R. (1991). Economic growth in a cross-section of countries. *Quarterly Journal of Economics, 106*, 407–443.

Barro, R. (1997). *Determinants of economic growth: A cross-country empirical study*. MIT Press.

Bloom, D., & Williamson, J. (1998). Demographic transition and economic miracles in emerging Asia. *World Bank Economic Review, 12*(3), 419–456.

Bloom, D., & Canning, D. (2004). Global demographic change: Dimensions and economic significance. In *Global Demographic Change: Economic Impacts and Policy Challenges. Proceedings of a Symposium Sponsored by the Federal Reserve Bank of Kansas City* (pp. 9–56). Jackson Hole.

Bloom, D., Canning, D., Fink, G., & Finlay, J. (2009). Fertility, female labor force participation, and the demographic dividend. *Journal of Economic Growth, 14*(2), 79–101.

Canning, D., Raja, S., & Yazbeck, A. (2015). *Africa's demographic transition: Dividend or disaster?* World Bank Group.

Coale, A., & Hoover, E. (1958). *Population growth and economic development in low-income countries: A case study of India's prospects*. Princeton University Press.

Cruz, M., Ahmed, S. (2016). *On the impact of demographic change on savings, growth, and poverty*. World Bank Policy Research Working Paper 7805. World Bank Group.

Eastwood, R., & Lipton, M. (2011). Demographic transition in sub-Saharan Africa: How big will the economic dividend be? *Population Studies, 65*(1), 9–35.

Hasan, R., Moucheraud, H., Samaha, S., Troiano, S., Ahmed, A., Osorio-Rodarte, I., Suzuki, E., Sexton, M., Pradhan, E., Madhavan, S., & Bou-Habib, C. (2019). *Demographic dividend in DRC: Catalyzing economic growth through demographic opportunities*. World Bank Group.

Headey, D., & Hodge, A. (2009). The effect of population growth on economic growth: A meta-regression analysis of the macroeconomic literature. *Population and Development Review, 35*(2), 221–248.

Higgins, M., & Williamson, J. (1997). Age structure dynamics in Asia and dependence on foreign capital. *Population and Development Review, 23*(2), 261–293.

Karra, M., Canning, D., Wilde, J. (2017). The effect of fertility decline on economic growth in Africa: A macrosimulation model. In J. B., Casterline & J. Bongaarts (Eds.), *Fertility transition in sub-Saharan Africa. Population and Development Review 43*(Suppl.), 237–263.

Kelley, A. (2001). The population debate in historical perspective: Revisionism revised. In N. Birdsall & S. S. Kelley (Eds.), *Population matters: Demographic change, economic growth, and poverty in the developing world* (pp. 24–54). Oxford University Press.

Kelley, A. (2005). Evolution of recent economic-demographic modeling: A synthesis. *Journal of Population Economics, 18*(2), 275–300.

References

Kelley, A., & Schmidt, R. (1995). Aggregate population and economic growth correlations: The role of the components of demographic change. *Demography, 32*(4), 543–555.

Kelley, A., & Schmidt, R. (2001) Economic and demographic change: A synthesis of models, findings, and perspectives. In N. Birdsall, A. Kelley & S. Sinding (Eds.), *Population matters: Demographic change, economic growth, and poverty in the developing world* (pp. 67–105). Oxford University Press.

Kelley, A., & Schmidt R. (2007). A century of demographic change and economic growth: The Asian experience in regional and temporal perspective. In A. Mason, & M. Yamaguchi, (Eds.), *Population change, labor markets and sustainable growth: Towards a new economic paradigm* (pp. 39–74). Amsterdam, NL: Elsevier.

Kuznets, S. (1967). Population and economic growth. *Proceedings of the American Philosophical Society, 111*(3), 170–193.

Lee, R., & Mason, A. (2006). What is the demographic dividend? *Finance and Development, 43*(3), 16–17.

Mason, A., & Kinugasa, T. (2008). East Asian economic development: Two demographic dividends. *Journal of Asian Economics, 19*(5), 389–399.

Mason, A., Lee, R., & XueJiang, J. (2016). Demographic dividends, human capital, and saving. *The Journal of the Economics of Ageing 7*, 106–122

Mason, A., Lee, R., Abrigo, M., & Sang-Hyop, L. (2017). Support ratios and demographic dividends: Estimates for the World. UN Population Division Technical Paper No. 2017/1. United Nations.

NAS. (1971). *Rapid population growth: Consequences and policy implications.* Johns Hopkins Press for the National Academies of Sciences.

National Research Council. (1986). *Population growth and economic development.* National Academy of Sciences.

Simon, J. (1981). *The ultimate resource.* Princeton University Press.

Starbird, E., Norton, M., & Marcus, R. (2016). Investing in family planning: Key to achieving the sustainable development goals. *Global Health: Science and Practice, 4*(2), 191–210.

United Nations Population Division. (2019). World population prospects 2019, Online Edition. Rev.1. Department of Economic and Social Affairs, United Nations, New York.

World Bank. (2016). *Global monitoring report 2015/2016: Development goals in an era of demographic change.* World Bank Group.

Open Access This chapter is licensed under the terms of the Creative Commons Attribution 4.0 International License (http://creativecommons.org/licenses/by/4.0/), which permits use, sharing, adaptation, distribution and reproduction in any medium or format, as long as you give appropriate credit to the original author(s) and the source, provide a link to the Creative Commons license and indicate if changes were made.

The images or other third party material in this chapter are included in the chapter's Creative Commons license, unless indicated otherwise in a credit line to the material. If material is not included in the chapter's Creative Commons license and your intended use is not permitted by statutory regulation or exceeds the permitted use, you will need to obtain permission directly from the copyright holder.

Chapter 7
The Impact of Voluntary Family Planning Programs on Contraceptive Use, Fertility, and Population

7.1 Introduction

When concern about the adverse impact of rapid population growth became widespread in the 1950 and 1960s, policy makers searched for interventions to slow growth. Family planning programs were an obvious choice, but there was significant doubt that these would work, because of the widely held belief that fertility would not decline until societies experienced significant, widespread social and economic change. Influential analysts argued that women in poor countries would not use contraception offered by programs because they wanted large families (Davis, 1967; Hauser, 1967). These doubts were allayed by findings from surveys which interviewed women about their reproductive preferences. Many women in Asia and Latin America (but not in SS Africa) wanted families of modest size (Lightbourne, 1987; Mauldin, 1965). Successful small experimental studies confirmed women's willingness to accept contraceptives, thus providing the scientific foundation for the family planning movement in subsequent decades (e.g., Fawcett, 1970; Foreit & Frejka, 1998; Freedman & Takeshita, 1969). From the late 1960s onward substantial funding from international sources became available to governments that were willing to start family planning programs (Donaldson, 1990; Piotrow, 1973). The availability of new methods (the pill, IUD, and new methods of sterilization) made the mass distribution of contraceptives more affordable and easier to implement. The family planning movement was particularly successful in Asia and North Africa (Robinson & Ross, 2007). In Latin America (and in the Philippines) opposition from the Catholic Church made governments reluctant to promote contraception, but large, well-funded NGOs (e.g., Profamilia in Columbia and BEMFAM in Brazil) took on the task of distributing family planning methods. In sub-Saharan Africa governments generally expressed little interest in family planning before the 1990s with notable exceptions of Botswana, Kenya, Ghana, and South Africa (May, 2017). In the 1990s the AIDS epidemic in large parts of the African continent put a damper on government investments in family planning. Everywhere the success of programs relied on strong support of government leaders. In the early 2000s several additional African countries implemented successful programs (e.g., Ethiopia, Malawi, Rwanda, and Zambia). Many other countries including Nigeria and the Democratic Republic of the Congo have made little progress in the development of strong programs.

7.2 The Role of Family Planning Programs in Removing Obstacles to the Use of Contraception

As noted in Chap. 3 the existence of large numbers of unplanned births and abortions in countries around the world is incontrovertible evidence that many women lack full control over their reproductive lives. Unplanned outcomes occur when sexually active women who want to avoid pregnancy either use no contraception or experience contraceptive failure. This is, in turn, largely the consequence of a wide range of social, health, and economic factors that pose barriers to women (and men) who wish to practice contraception (Bongaarts & Bruce, 1995; Bongaarts et al., 2012; Casterline et al., 1997; Casterline & Sinding, 2000; Casterline et al., 2001; Cleland, 2001; Cleland et al., 2006; El-Zanaty et al., 1999; Cleland forthcoming).

The main obstacles identified by researchers include:

Lack of knowledge. To use a modern method, women must be aware of its existence, and they must know how to use the method, and where to obtain supplies. Knowledge of at least one modern method was very limited in the 1950 and 1960s in the developing world, but by the early 1990s became widespread in Asia and Latin America and in a number of countries in SSA (Curtis et al., 1996).

Availability of family planning methods. A couple must have access to a contraceptive method to adopt it. For traditional methods such as abstinence and withdrawal no source is required (but partner cooperation is needed); and for permanent methods such as sterilization, one-time access suffices. But for widely used modern methods such as injectables, condoms and the pill, a dependable source within a reasonable distance is needed. The density of these access points varies widely among and within countries. Access is most difficult in rural communities in countries where family planning programs are absent or weak and is particularly problematic when traditional customs restrict women's mobility.

Costs. While physical proximity is important, services must be reasonably priced. The direct cost of commodities (e.g., pills, injection, condoms, IUDs), transportation, and provider fees for contraceptives and health care services can be substantial. As a result, poor women are often unable to afford modern methods without the subsidies provided by family planning programs.

Quality of services. To satisfy clients, services must be of adequate quality. This includes the provision of a choice of methods, a well-trained staff and the respectful treatment of clients. Most women prefer female providers.

Health concerns and side effects. Health concerns and fear of side effects are two of the most commonly expressed reasons for nonuse and for discontinuing the use of contraception. Choosing a method often involves weighing a variety of drawbacks to find the method that is least objectionable. The most serious health effects are cardiovascular complications of the pill; pelvic inflammatory disease, uterine perforation, and anemia for the IUD; and infections associated with sterilization and other methods. These complications are uncommon if users are well informed and service providers are well trained and have access to appropriate

7.2 The Role of Family Planning Programs in Removing Obstacles ...

equipment and drugs. Physiological effects (e.g., nausea, headache, weight gain, menstrual changes) associated with some contraceptive methods also influence women's choices.

Still other drawbacks play potentially significant roles in the decision to adopt a method. For example, manipulation of genitals or interruption of intercourse is required for the use of the condom, diaphragm, cap, sponge, and spermicides. Many women dislike the physical exams (often performed by male providers) required for IUD insertions and for fitting the diaphragm and caps. Others fear the surgical procedures associated with sterilization and implants. Loss of potency is a concern for some men who might otherwise consider a vasectomy. Many of these health concerns are based on or exaggerated by rumors and misinformation.

Objections from husbands or other family members. For many married women, objections to family planning from their husbands or partners is a sufficient reason not to practice contraception, despite their desire to do so. Other family members (e.g., parents or parents-in-law) or neighbors may also discourage the practice of contraception. Reasons for these objections may include the desire for more children than the women herself wants, costs of contraceptive supply and associated health care, concerns about side effects, and moral or religious beliefs. In traditional societies, family limitation and negotiation over sexual matters may not be considered respectable subjects.

Concerns about moral and social acceptability. In nearly every society the introduction of the idea of birth control and the methods used to achieve it meet resistance from political, church, and medical leaders. Family planning was viewed as usurping divine will, encouraging promiscuity leading to a breakdown of family life, and threating individual health and national vitality (Cleland, 2001). Such forms of resistance were common in Europe in the late nineteenth century, and resistance remains common in many contemporary developing countries. Sometimes the opposition is embodied in formal religious doctrine (e.g., the Roman Catholic ban on artificial methods and the Islamic opposition to sterilization). Up to the 1970s most African leaders had a mercantilist view of population: larger populations were better than smaller populations and rapid growth was better than slow growth. In Latin America the early enthusiasm for family planning revolved around limiting unsafe abortion rather than reducing fertility or population growth. It was not until about 1980 that the benefits of fertility decline, and smaller families became widely accepted by government leaders and the general population.

These obstacles to adoption of contraception are the main cause of unplanned pregnancies. Removing these barriers is, therefore, the goal of voluntary family planning programs. The primary task of family planning programs is to offer women and couples easy access to a wide range of affordable, reliable, and high-quality contraceptive methods and related services. To achieve this objective, many countries have built service delivery networks that may include hospitals, health and family planning centers, work-based clinics, mobile medical and paramedical units, community-based distribution, and commercial outlets. Contraceptives are usually provided at low cost or for free. The most effective programs have minimized access obstacles by training female outreach workers who visit women in their homes.

To be successful in helping women and couples avoid unintended pregnancies, family planning programs must go beyond simply providing physical access to contraceptive supplies and reduce or eliminate the other obstacles to contraceptive use noted above (Cleland et al., 2012; Cleland forthcoming). A number of approaches can address these barriers, including: (1) education campaigns through mass media, called IEC (information, education, and communication) or BCC (behavioral change communication); (2) training service providers to increase their knowledge and to encourage improvements in the quality of services; (3) increasing women's empowerment and agency; (4) collaboration with community leaders; and (5) ensuring that others with significant influence on women's contraceptive behavior (e.g., husbands, partners, mothers-in-law) have accurate information about family planning and the costs and benefits of childbearing.

The final ingredient of a successful family planning program is strong support from government leaders at the local and national level. This support can be encouraged by providing regular briefings on program progress and on the social and economic benefits of contraceptive use and lower fertility. It is also crucial to collaborate with policymakers to remove or revise laws, regulations, official guidelines and other structural factors that are barriers to contraceptive adoption and distribution.

By providing access to high-quality contraceptive services, addressing barriers to use, and ensuring political support, family planning programs can maximize adoption of contraception among women who want to space or limit their births. Information and education campaigns about the benefits of smaller families also play an important role in increasing overall demand for contraception, as will be demonstrated below.

7.3 Program Impact on Contraceptive Use

Well-designed family planning programs can help women implement their fertility preferences and reduce unintended births and abortions. A number of evaluations of these programs have found that they can have a significant impact on contraceptive use and fertility (Ahlburg & Diamond, 1996; Bongaarts, 1997, 2020; Bongaarts & Hardee, 2019; Miller & Babiarz, 2016; Tsui, 2001). However, other studies (in particular, Pritchett, 1994) conclude that family planning programs have a minimal impact on reproductive behavior. We will examine this controversy in more detail, beginning with a summary of the evidence that family planning programs have an impact on fertility.

Three different approaches have been used to obtain estimates of family planning programs' impact across a wide range of periods and contexts.

7.3.1 Controlled Experiments

Controlled experiments are the gold standard for evaluating interventions, but very few large-scale experiments have been conducted to assess family planning programs, in part because they are expensive and take a long time to complete. The largest and most influential of these experiments is the Family Planning and Health Services Project (FPHSP), started in the late 1970s in Matlab, a rural district in Bangladesh (Cleland et al., 1994; Phillips et al., 1982, 1988). At the time FPHSP started, Bangladesh was one of the poorest and most highly agricultural countries in the world, and there was widespread skepticism that family planning would be accepted

7.3 Program Impact on Contraceptive Use

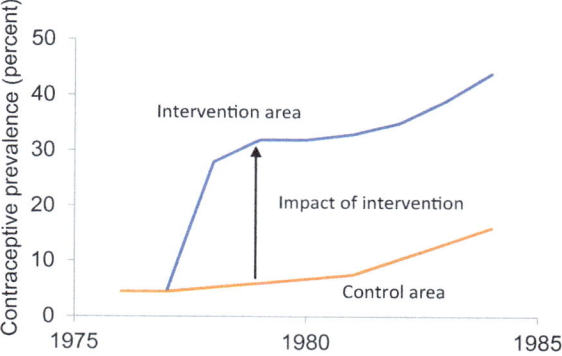

Fig. 7.1 Contraceptive use trends in family planning experiment in Matlab, Bangladesh (Phillips et al., 1988; Cleland et al., 1994)

in such a traditional society. The FPHSP divided the Matlab district (population of 173,000 in 1977) into experimental and control areas of approximately equal size. The control area received the same services as the rest of the country. In the 1970s these services were very limited and did not significantly affect contraceptive use. In the experimental area comprehensive high-quality family planning services were provided, aimed at reducing the costs (monetary, social, psychological, and health) of adopting contraception. In the experimental area women were provided with free services and supplies of modern contraceptive methods; home visits by well-trained female family planning workers; regular follow-up to address health concerns; information campaigns; menstrual regulation services; and outreach to husbands, community leaders, and religious leaders to address potential social and familial objections from men.

The impact of the program was large and immediate (Cleland et al., 1994; Phillips et al., 1988). As shown in Fig. 7.1, within two years, modern contraceptive use increased from five to 33% among married women in the experimental area while little change occurred in the control area. The experiment left no doubt that a well-designed family planning program could be successful in a very poor, largely illiterate, agricultural society. Its success led the Bangladesh government to implement a nation-wide family planning program that employed many of the innovations from the Matlab, such as house-to-house visits by well-trained young female community health workers (Cleland et al., 1994).

7.3.2 Natural Experiments

Unlike controlled experiments, which are carefully designed and implemented to evaluate a particular intervention, 'natural experiments' take advantage of existing diversity and compare two populations with similar social, economic, cultural, and religious characteristics, but with differing approaches to family planning. Differences between such populations in contraceptive use and fertility demonstrate the

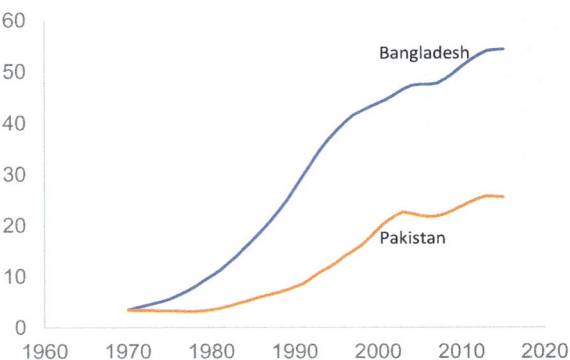

Fig. 7.2 Contraceptive prevalence (modern) in Bangladesh and Pakistan, 1970–2015 (United Nations, 2021)

potential effects of voluntary family planning (Bongaarts et al., 2012; Cleland, 1994; Lee et al., 1998).

One of the best-known examples of a natural experiment is the comparison of Bangladesh and Pakistan, which were one country from independence in 1947 until 1971. Both had similar cultures and levels of social and economic development. However, the countries differed remarkably in their commitment to voluntary family planning. Following the Matlab experiment, Bangladesh, starting around 1980, implemented one of the world's most comprehensive national family planning programs based on the Matlab model, while Pakistan's program lacked government funds and commitment and remained weak and relatively ineffective (Cleland & Lush, 1997).

Figure 7.2 plots the contraceptive prevalence rate among married women (mCPR) from 1970 to 2015 for the two countries. Both started at very low levels in 1970 and rose over time, but the increase in Bangladesh was substantially larger than in Pakistan. By 2015 the gap had reached almost 30% points (54.3% vs. 25.6%). The most recent Demographic and Health Survey conducted in 2017–2018 suggests that Pakistan's mCPR leveled off in the mid-2010s (NIPS-Pakistan & ICF, 2019).

Previous examinations of the Pakistan-Bangladesh difference in reproductive behavior have also attributed it largely to the much higher quality family planning program in Bangladesh (Cleland & Lush, 1997).

Other natural experiments lead to broadly similar conclusions (Bongaarts et al. forthcoming). Rwanda and Burundi are poor, densely populated countries in East Africa with comparable socio-economic profiles. Rwanda's family planning program is much stronger than Burundi's leading to mCPR gap in 2015 of 24.1% points (47.2% vs. 23.1%). Ethiopia and Nigeria are the two largest countries in SSA. The former has an effective family planning program while the latter does not. As a result, Ethiopia's mCPR (36.0%) exceeds Nigeria's (10.8%) by 25.3% points (United Nations Population Division, 2021).

The three natural experiments had comparable results with mCPR gaps in 2015 of 28.7% points for Bangladesh-Pakistan, 24.1% points for Rwanda-Burundi and 25.3% points for Ethiopia-Nigeria.

7.3.3 Natural Experiments: Adjusted Results

These comparisons of three country pairs should be regarded as approximations of the impact of strong versus weak family planning programs because the levels of development in the countries in each pair are not exactly the same. In the absence of family planning programs in both countries of each pair their levels of contraceptive use might still be different in 2015 because socio-economic conditions differ. To address this issue, we continue the analysis of natural experiments but control for the level of education when comparing the countries. As noted in Chap. 4, education is by far the most influential socio-economic determinant of fertility. Taking its potential confounding effect into account should lead to more accurate results from the natural experiments.

Figure 7.3 plots the mCPR of Bangladesh and Pakistan by level of education from 1970 to 2015. The figure looks like Fig. 7.2, which is not surprising because the values of all plotted points are the same. But there is a crucial difference between the two figures: In Fig. 7.2 each observation for each country is plotted in the corresponding year, which is measured along the horizontal axis. In Fig. 7.3 the horizontal axis measures the level of education in the corresponding year. For example, the last point (A) in the graph for Bangladesh is the 2015 level of mCPR (54.3%) which is plotted at 6.4 years of education. For Pakistan the mCPR in 2015 is estimates at 25.6 (point C) but in that year the level of education was 5.0 years, significantly below the level in Bangladesh. Pakistan's mCPR is lower than Bangladesh's not only because of its weaker program but also because of its lower level of education.

To assess the family planning program impact without the confounding effect of education we must compare the two countries when they were at the same level of education. In this case we compare the two countries at an education level of 5 years of schooling, which gives a mCPR of 26 for Pakistan in 2015 and 49 for Bangladesh in 2007 (points C and B in Fig. 7.3). The education-adjusted gap between the two

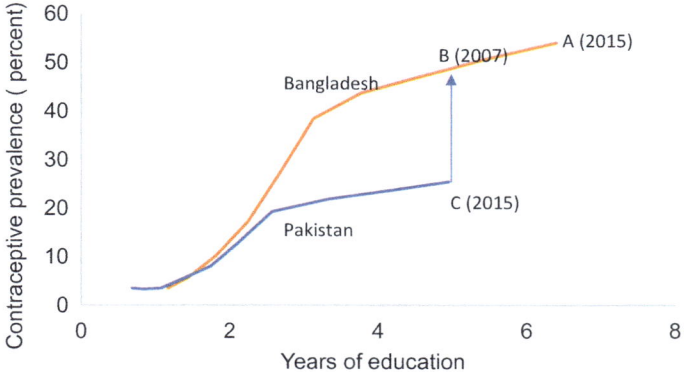

Fig. 7.3 Contraceptive prevalence by education, Bangladesh and Pakistan, 1970–2015 (United Nations, 2021; Wittgenstein Center, 2021)

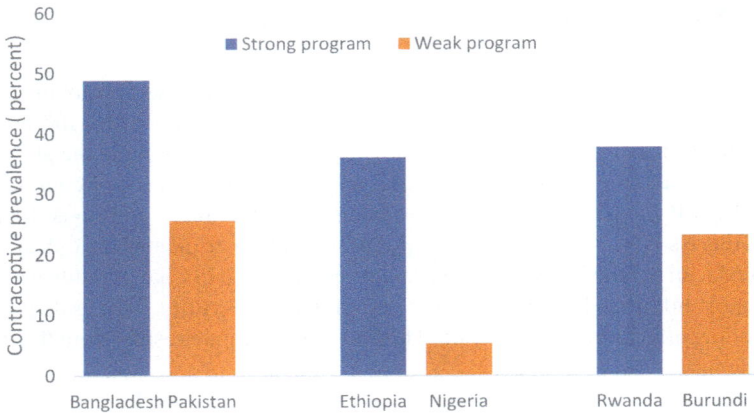

Fig. 7.4 Education adjusted mCPR in 2015 for three pairs of countries with strong/weak family planning programs (Authors' calculations from United Nations, 2021)

countries therefore is 23% points (49–26) rather than the unadjusted gap of 29% points obtained from Fig. 7.2.

Figure 7.4 presents education adjusted results for the natural experiments in three pairs of countries Bangladesh-Pakistan, Ethiopia-Nigeria, Rwanda-Burundi. The results for the adjusted mCPR gap between the country with the strongest and weakest program countries are, respectively 23, 31 and 15% points for married women.

These findings from natural experiments are informative but do not provide accurate estimates of the full family planning program impact. Instead, these comparisons provide an estimate of the *difference* between the weaker and stronger programs and do not give an estimate of the *total* program impact of the strong program country, because the weaker programs have some effect that cannot be ignored. To address this issue, we turn to regression analysis.

7.3.4 Regressions: Program Impact on Contraceptive Use, Demand, and Satisfaction

In the absence of experimental evidence for most countries, researchers have relied on regression analysis to estimate the effects of family planning programs on the level and pattern of fertility. As noted earlier, the extensive literature on the determinants of fertility identifies two general factors as the main determinants of fertility declines in the developing world over the past half century: socio-economic development, in particular education, and family planning programs. Regression analyses have been used to estimate the separate impact of development versus family programs on contraceptive use and fertility change (Ahlburg & Diamond, 1996; Bongaarts, 1998, 2020; Bongaarts & Hardee, 2019; Miller & Babiarz, 2016; Pritchett, 1994; Tsui,

2001). In these regressions, contraceptive use or fertility are the dependent variables and the independent variables consist of one or more socio-economic indicators, plus an indicator of family planning program effort.

A key issue in these regressions is measurement of the strength of a program in a country, which is not straightforward. The oldest indicator is the Family Planning Program Effort (FPE) score, which has been used since the early 1970s to gauge the strength of national programs (Kuang & Brodsky, 2016; Ross & Smith, 2011). To obtain this score, knowledgeable observers in each country answer questions about a variety of program characteristics and policy actions. Their responses are combined to yield an overall FPE score. Over the past three decades, the FPE score for countries has been measured in eight cycles ending in 2014.

The FPE scores suffers from some shortcomings. Differences among countries and across cycles can occur simply because the experts often must make subjective assessments and the experts change over time. In addition, the questions included in the index have been refined and changed over time. As a result, differences between FPE scores of countries and trends for individual countries should be interpreted with caution.

More recently, Bongaarts and Hardee (2017) have proposed an alternative program indicator called *Public-sector family planning program impact score* to measure the quality and scope of a government sponsored family planning program. We will refer to this variable as the 'program score' (PS). It equals the product of two other variables: (1) the proportion of demand that is satisfied by modern methods; and (2) the proportion of modern methods that is provided by the public sector. PS therefore equals the proportion of all demand that is satisfied with modern methods from the public sector. This score, which can be consistently measured over time in countries with Demographic and Health Surveys (DHS), does not rely on subjective assessments. It ranges from zero in the absence of a government program to a theoretical value of 100 for the strongest public programs where all demand for contraception is met by the public sector. A country can have low demand and a low mCPR but a high PS if the mCPR is close to the demand and all contraception is provided by the public sector. Conversely, a country can have high demand and a high mCPR but a low PS if the public sector is small and contraceptives are mostly provided through the private sector.

To provide a first look at the relationship between education, program score, and contraceptive use, we plot in Fig. 7.5 the prevalence of modern contraception (mCPR) by the mean years of schooling among women aged 20–39. The figure contains 22 markers, one for each of 22 largest countries in SSA, representing observations at the most recent DHS (ca. 2013). The size of the round marker is proportional to the program score of the country which ranges from 5 in Congo DR to 62 in Zimbabwe.

If female education were the only determinant of the mCPR, the observations for all countries would fall on a single upward sloping line. This is clearly not the case, indicating an impact of family planning programs and other factors. In general, the higher the level of women's educational attainment and the higher the program score, the higher the mCPR. A key finding is that at any level of women's educational attainment, the mCPR varies widely. For example, in the countries with

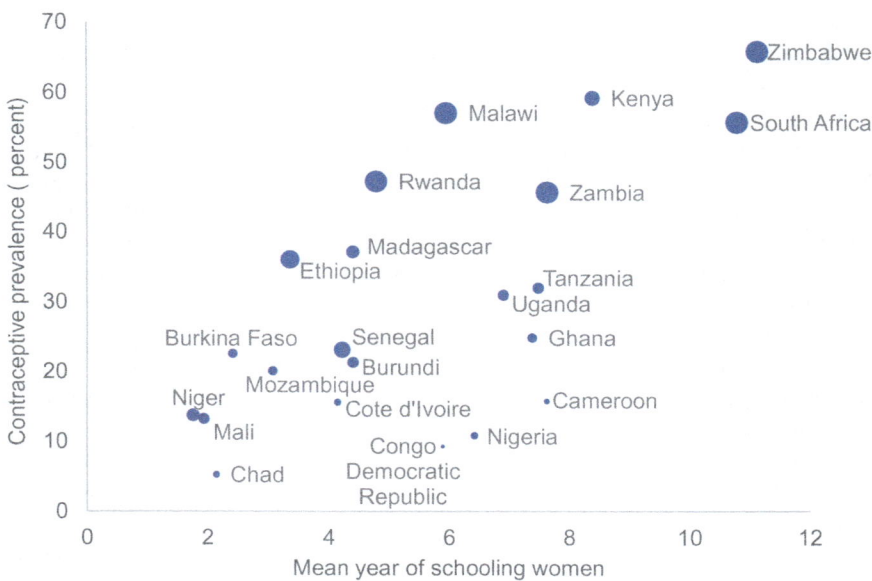

Fig. 7.5 Contraceptive prevalence by mean years of schooling and program score (circle), 22 sub-Saharan Countries 2015 (United Nations Population Division, 2021; Wittgenstein Center, 2021)

average schooling levels around six years, the mCPR ranges from 9% in Congo DR to 57% in Malawi. As will be shown below, the differences among countries with similar levels of women's educational attainment are to a large extent the result of program differences. The findings in Fig. 7.5 suggest that education and program score both have a substantial effect on mCPR, but quantifying these effects requires formal regression analysis.

Our regression analysis of mCPR trends in SSA is an updated and expanded version of one carried out by Bongaarts and Hardee (2019). The regressions focus on sub-Saharan Africa because most countries in this continent are still in their fertility transitions and many governments have made only limited investments in family planning programs. The debate about the impact of family planning programs is clearly especially relevant in this continent. In addition, the program score was designed for use in SSA, and can be biased in other continents where the private sector has become the dominant provider of services, often with the assistance of governments.

Three regression models are presented below, with mCPR, the demand for contraception, and the satisfaction of demand as the three dependent variables. Each regression has two explanatory variables: (1) education as measured by the average years of schooling among women aged 20–39 ('education'); and (2) program score, PS. In Chap. 4 education was found to be the dominant socio-economic determinant of fertility especially in SSA. (Adding other socio-economic indicators yielded no new significant coefficients.) The regressions rely on data from 33 countries in SSA with

7.3 Program Impact on Contraceptive Use

Table 7.1 Results of fixed effects regression models of contraceptive prevalence on socio-economic variables on in 33 sub-Saharan Africa countries with two or more DHS surveys after 1990

Model 1: mCPR		
	Coefficient	p
Education	2.29	0.000
Program score	0.64	0.000
Constant	−5.50	0.01
R^2	0.91	
Model 2: Demand for contraception		
Education	1.65	0.01
Program score	0.30	0.000
Constant	36.5	0.000
R^2	0.63	
Model 3: Satisfaction of demand		
Education	3.77	0.01
Program score	0.91	0.000
Constant	−3.55	0.000
R^2	0.93	

at least two Demographic and Health Surveys after 1990 and with a population size above one million. Data from all available DHSs in each country are included (ICF International, 2021) for a total 133 surveys. By using countries as their own controls, fixed effects models account for time-stable differences among countries, which may otherwise introduce bias into parameter estimation.

Model 1 in Table 7.1 presents the results for the regression of the determinants of mCPR. The coefficients for women's education and PS are highly significant, thus confirming their impact on contraceptive prevalence. A year of education raises mCPR by 2.29% and a point increase in the PS raises the mCPR by 0.64%.

Figure 7.6 plots the country specific estimates of the total program impact at the time of the most recent DHS survey. Each estimate is obtained by multiplying the PS regression coefficient of 0.64 by the observed value of the PS in each country. The biggest program impacts, exceeding 30%, were found in South Africa, Zimbabwe, Zambia, Rwanda, Malawi, Namibia, and Ethiopia. In contrast, the program impact was less than 5% in Cote d'Ivoir, Congo and the Democratic Republic of the Congo.

Models 2 and 3 in Table 7.1 present results from the fixed effects regressions for demand and for the satisfaction of demand. The effects of education and the program score are statistically significant in both models. For example, in Model 3 the coefficient for the program effect on percent of demand satisfied equals 0.91. This means that a 50% change in PS on average leads to an increase of 45% in the percent of demand satisfied. The family planning program score also affects demand for contraception, but with a smaller coefficient of 0.30. In other words, PS affects contraceptive prevalence by raising both demand and the level of satisfaction, with the latter being three times more important than the former.

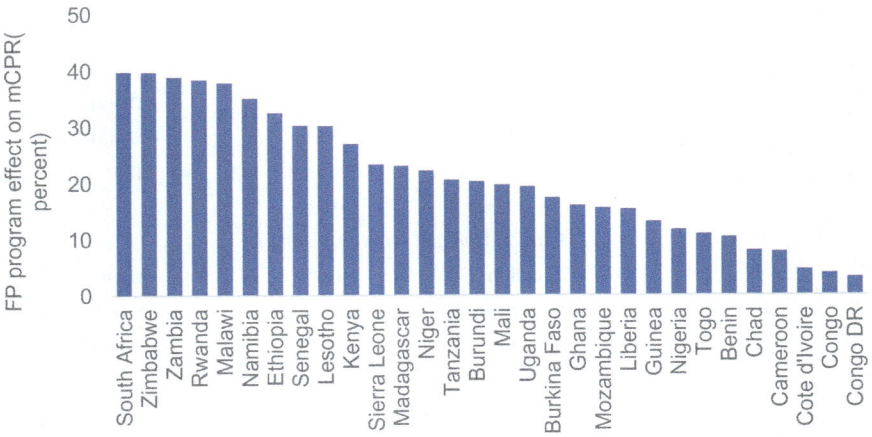

Fig. 7.6 Impact of family planning program on modern contraceptive prevalence

The three different approaches to estimating the mCPR impact of the highest-quality family planning programs yield the following results: (1) 28% for the controlled experiment in Matlab; (2) 15–31% for differences between stronger and weaker programs in 'natural experiment' comparisons of countries; and (3) 30–40% for the absolute effects of the strongest programs in SSA in regression analyses. These findings are broadly consistent with one another. However, the first and second approaches underestimate the absolute program effect and just estimate the difference between weak and strong programs, thus ignoring any program effect in the weaker program countries or control area. The regression approach does not have this bias and can therefore be expected to yield somewhat higher program impact estimates on the mCPR.

7.4 Program Impact on Fertility

The three different approaches to estimating the program impact on contraceptive prevalence can also provide estimates of the program impact on fertility.

7.4.1 Controlled Experiments

As shown in the preceding section, contraceptive use in the experimental area of Matlab rose sharply while little change occurred in the control area. One would therefore expect a more rapid fertility decline in the experimental than in the control area. This was exactly what was observed: a difference of 25% (around 1.5 births

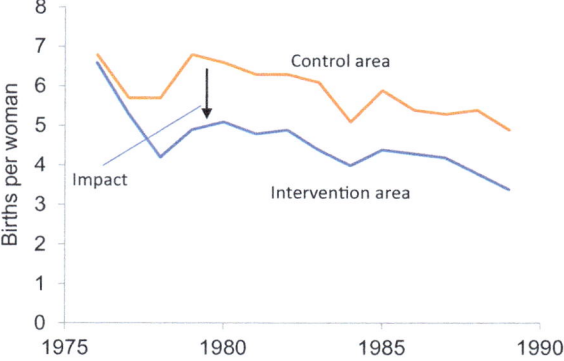

Fig. 7.7 Fertility impact of family planning experiment in Matlab, Bangladesh (ICDDR, 1994, 2001; Phillips et al., 1982)

per woman) was maintained through the 1980s until the services in the control area and in the rest of the country were also improved (see Fig. 7.7).

A similar but more complex quasi-experimental study was conducted in the Navrongo district of Northern Ghana in the 1990s, where over a third of women wanted to space or limit additional births but few were using contraception. Though direct estimates of changes in contraceptive use from the Navrongo project are not available, an evaluation found that the project led to improved knowledge and use of modern contraception and to a decline in the TFR of one birth per woman in the initial three years of the project, a 15% decline in fertility relative to comparison areas (Debpuur et al., 2002).

7.4.2 Natural Experiments

As expected, the differences in mCPR trends between Bangladesh and Pakistan since 1970 have led to differences in fertility transitions. In 1970 the TFR was close to 7 births per women in both countries, a level that had probably not changed significantly for many decades. In the 1980s the TFRs began to diverge (see Fig. 7.8) and by 2015 the gap between the two countries reached 1.6 births per woman (3.7 vs. 2.1).

Natural experiments in other countries yield broadly similar results. Ethiopia and Nigeria, and Rwanda and Burundi are pairs of countries with comparable socio-economic profiles. The TFRs declined to substantially lower levels in countries with stronger programs (Ethiopia and Rwanda) than in corresponding weaker program countries (Nigeria and Burundi). The 2015 difference between the TFRs of the stronger and weaker program countries ranged from 1.0 birth per woman for Ethiopia-Nigeria pair to 1.5 births per woman for the Rwanda-Burundi pair.

Fig. 7.8 Total fertility rate 1970–2015 Bangladesh and Pakistan (United Nations, 2019)

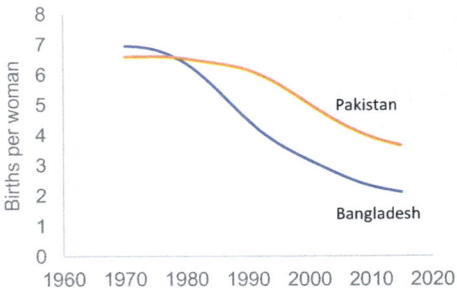

7.4.3 Natural Experiments: Adjusted Results

The TFR results from these natural experiments are confounded by differences in socio-economic development between the countries in each pair. To address this issue, we introduce a control for the level of education in all countries. As discussed in Chap. 4 education of females is the most important determinant of fertility decline.

The adjustment procedure used for the mCPR can also be applied to obtain an estimate of the education adjusted gap for the TFR. Figure 7.9 plots the TFR of Bangladesh and Pakistan by level of education from 1970 to 2015. In 2015 the TFRs of the two countries differed by 1.6 births per woman. But at the education level of five years of schooling, the gap is just 1.1 births per woman. The education adjustment clearly reduces the gap.

This, however, is not the whole story because there is another bias. As is clear from Fig. 7.9, Bangladesh started off in 1970 at a higher fertility level than Pakistan. To assess the impact of relative impact of the programs we must take this different starting point into account. We do this by comparing the *declines* in fertility of the two countries between the first and last points where a comparison is possible (i.e., at education levels of 1.4 and 5.0 years, respectively). At the education level of 1.4 Bangladesh's fertility is higher than Pakistan's by 0.4 births per woman and at the education level of 5 the gap is 1.1. The decline is 4.4 births per woman in Bangladesh and 2.8 in Pakistan. The difference in declines is therefore 1.6 births

Fig. 7.9 Total fertility rate by level of education, 1970–2015, Bangladesh and Pakistan (Authors' calculations; United Nations, 2019)

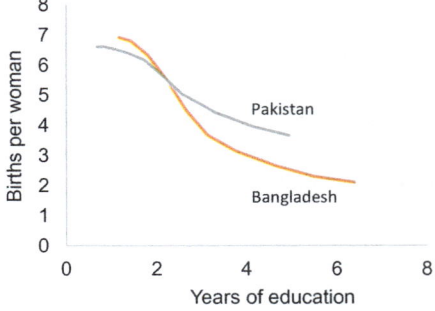

7.4 Program Impact on Fertility

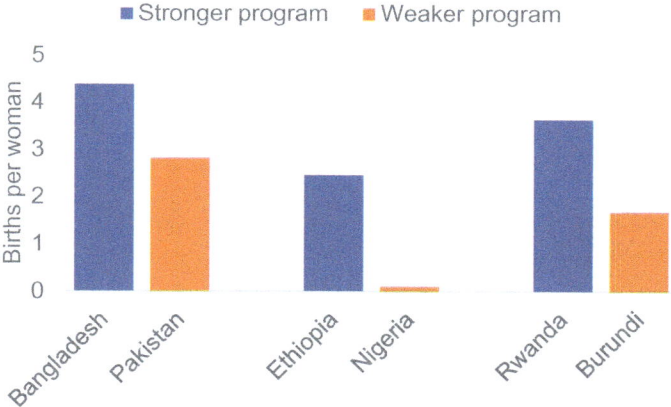

Fig. 7.10 Education adjusted declines in TFR: stronger versus weaker program countries (Authors' calculations; United Nations, 2019)

per woman. This gap might be the result of the difference in the strengths of family planning programs in Bangladesh and Pakistan (in the early 2000s the PS score of the two countries equaled 39 and 19 respectively). Differences in other socio-economic conditions that grew over time also had an impact but the adjustment for level of education minimizes their role.

Figure 7.10 presents education adjusted declines for the natural experiments in three pairs of countries: Bangladesh-Pakistan, Ethiopia-Nigeria, Rwanda-Burundi. The adjusted TFR gaps in declines are 1.6, 2.4 and 2.0 births per woman, respectively, which might be attributable to differences in the strength of family planning programs.

7.4.4 Regressions: Program Impact on Fertility

The regression analyses of fertility declines rely on the same methodology as the regression analyses of the mCPR presented above. The determinants of fertility and its wanted and unwanted components in SSA will be assessed by relying on fixed effect regressions using country-level data from all DHS surveys in 33 countries with at least two such surveys. Table 7.2 presents the results of four models:

Model 1: The determinants of the TFR

The two independent variables included in Model 1 are women's education and the family planning program score. The coefficients for both variables are highly significant. On average, an increase of one year in school reduces the TFR by 0.185 births per woman and one point increase in the family planning score reduces the TFR by 0.025 births per woman.

Table 7.2 Results of fixed effects regression models of total fertility rate on education and program effort in 33 countries in sub-Saharan Africa

Model 1: TFR

	Coefficient	p
Education	−0.185	0.000
Program score	−0.025	0.000
Constant	6.80	0.000
R^2	0.51	

Model 2: Wanted TFR

Education	−0.215	0.000
Program score	0.016	0.001
Constant	5.7	0.000
R^2	0.55	

Model 3: Unwanted TFR

Education	0.03	0.504
Program score	−0.01	0.011
Constant	1.05	0.000
R^2	0.02	

Model 4: Unwanted TFR (2)

Education	−0.067	0.099
Program score	−0.016	0.000
Wanted TFR	−0.452	0.000
Constant	−3.64	0.000
R^2	0.39	

Model 2: the determinants of wanted TFR

The coefficients for education and program score are both highly significant and negative as expected on theoretical grounds. On average, one year of education reduces wanted fertility by 0.215 births per woman and one point in the PS score reduces the wanted TFR (WTFR) by 0.016 births per woman.

Model 3: the determinants of unwanted TFR

Model 3 repeats Models 1 and 2 except that the dependent variable is unwanted fertility (UWTFR). The results show a significant effect of program score but not for education. The latter finding is surprising because educated women generally have more knowledge about and access to contraception and have higher opportunity costs associated with an unwanted birth. The explanation for this unexpected finding lies in the process discussed in Chap. 3. Model 3 produces biased effects because it ignores the potential confounding effect of declining wanted fertility on unwanted fertility. As wanted fertility declines the potential number of unwanted births rises. Improvements in education and family planning programs have an uphill battle to overcome this rising level of potential unwanted fertility. The result of these competing factors is a non-significant effect for education and a relatively small but significant effect for family planning.

Model 4: the determinants of unwanted TFR with control for wanted TF

To reveal the unbiased effect of education and family planning score it is necessary to control for the confounding effect of declining wanted fertility. This is the objective of model 4 which is the same as model 3 except that wanted fertility is added as a third explanatory variable. As expected, model 4 results show a highly significant inverse effect of WTFR. In addition, the effects of education and family planning program are larger than in model 3 and are statistically significant (at the 10% level for education). The coefficient for the effect of program score on unwanted fertility (-0.016) is the same as for the effect on wanted fertility.

To provide further insight into these regression results we calculate the absolute effects of women's schooling and the family planning program on the TFR in each country. This effect can be estimated by multiplying the regression coefficients in model 1 by the observed values of the two explanatory variables. Figure 7.11 plots the resulting fertility effects in countries with a population over 5 million at the time of the most recent DHS survey. The average education effect (1.04 births per woman) exceeds the average program effect (0.84 births per woman). There is considerable variation among countries. For example, the education effect exceeds 1.5 birth per woman in Kenya, South Africa and Zimbabwe, but is less than 0.5 in Mozambique, Burkina Faso, Mali, Niger, and Chad. The countries with the highest program effects (around 1.5 births per woman) are Malawi, Rwanda, South Africa, Zimbabwe, and Zambia.[1]

The three different approaches to estimating the fertility impact of family planning programs yields comparable results: a reduction of 1.5 births per woman over a reproductive lifetime in the Matlab experiment, 1.6 to 2.4 births per woman in countries involved in the natural experiments, and around 1.5 in the countries in SSA with the highest family planning program scores.

7.5 Program Impact on Population Trends

By addressing the reproductive needs of couples, family planning programs raise contraceptive prevalence. This in turn reduces fertility and population growth, changes the age structure, and increases the demographic dividend.

To illustrate, we compare fertility and population trends in Pakistan and Bangladesh. In 1975–1980, the two countries had nearly the same high fertility near 7 births per woman, but, as seen above, trends diverged in subsequent decades, with more rapid declines in Bangladesh than in Pakistan. By 2015, Bangladesh's

---

[1] These regression results are slightly different from those presented in Bongaarts (2020). The main reason for this difference is that Bongaarts (2020) uses the standard DHS calculation for wanted fertility while the present study relies on a different approach proposed by Bongaarts (1990).

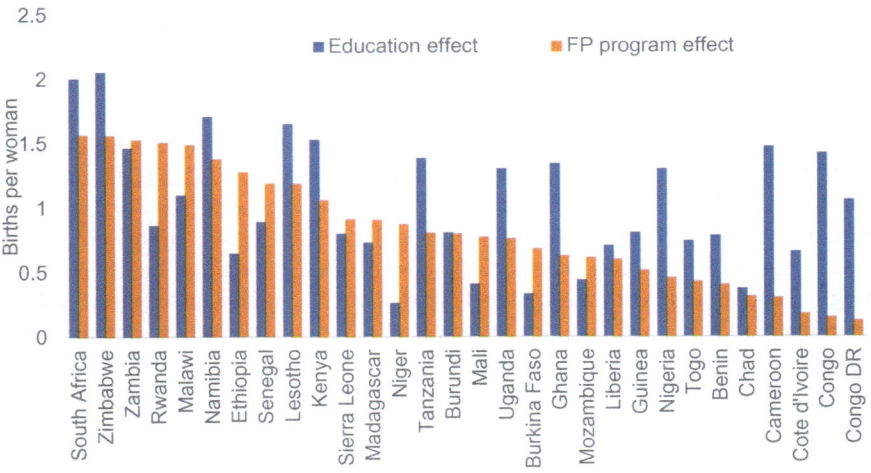

Fig. 7.11 Education and family planning program effects on TFR decline

fertility declined to 2.1 births per woman, while in Pakistan fertility stood at 3.7, a difference of 1.6 births per woman.

The different fertility trajectories resulted in increasingly large differences in population size over time (see Fig. 7.12). In 1980, the two populations were virtually the same size (about 80 million), but by 2100, Pakistan's population is projected to be more than double the size of Bangladesh's (403 vs. 151 million) (United Nations, 2019). This suggests that the Bangladesh family planning program led to a large reduction in the country's potential 2100 population.[2] Fertility and population trends are also affected by levels of socio-economic development, but this is unlikely to be the main explanation for the different population trajectories. Development levels, as measured by years of education, were similar in the 1970s in Bangladesh and Pakistan, which were and still are largely poor agricultural majority-Muslim countries. But over time education differences have appeared with education levels in 2015 reaching 6.4 years in Bangladesh and 5.0 years in Pakistan. This would be expected because one of the benefits of more rapid fertility decline is greater investments in education. It might therefore be argued that at least some of the education advantage of Bangladesh is due to earlier investments in its family planning program and the resulting demographic dividend (see Chap. 6).

The different fertility trajectories of Pakistan and Bangladesh also affect trends in the age structure and the demographic dividend. Figure 7.13 plots the proportion of working age people for the two countries from 1970 to 2015. After 1980 (the onset

---

[2] The difference in population projections is partly due to more rapid future life expectancy improvements in Bangladesh than in Pakistan. The UN's constant mortality projections yield populations sizes of 344 million for Pakistan and 120 million for Bangladesh. This finding indicates that differences in fertility trends are the dominant cause of differences in population projections to 2100.

7.5 Program Impact on Population Trends

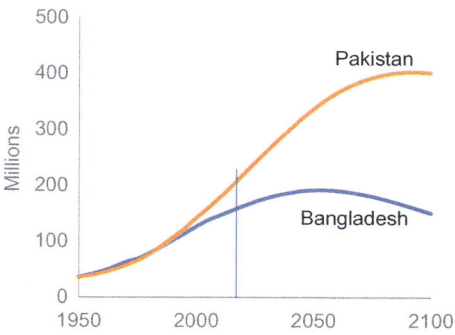

Fig. 7.12 Population Projections Bangladesh and Pakistan (United Nations, 2019)

of fertility decline in Bangladesh), the working age proportion of the population grew substantially faster in Bangladesh than in Pakistan. The economy also grew faster in Bangladesh than in Pakistan after 1990 (World Bank, 2021). There are, of course, other factors that contributed to the more rapid growth in Bangladesh, but the demographic tailwind was no doubt a key factor.

As noted earlier, the potential for a demographic dividend in SSA lies mostly in the future. To assess the potential demographic impact of a substantial investment in family planning programs in Africa, we compare the high and low variants of the UN population projections for SS Africa (United Nations Population Division, 2019). The difference between these two variants is the fertility level assumed in the future: the high variant exceeds the low variant by one birth per woman. Such a one-birth decline is achievable with the implementation of a high-quality family planning program (in fact Sect. 7.4 suggests the effect could be around 1.5 births per woman).

According to the medium variant, the population of SSA will quadruple in size from one billion in 2015 to 3.8 billion in 2100 (see Fig. 7.14). This projection assumes a steady decline in fertility and includes the impact of the AIDS epidemic. The high variant (with fertility a half birth higher than in the medium variant) projects 5.2 billion people in 2100. This trajectory could well become reality if no significant further investments are made in family planning, because past fertility declines have

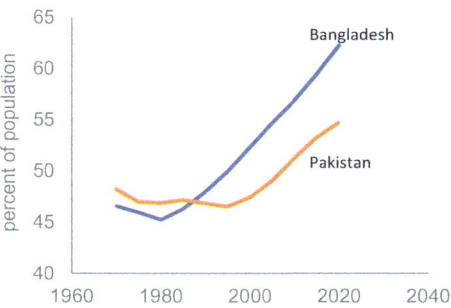

Fig. 7.13 Percent of population aged 18–64, Bangladesh and Pakistan (United Nations, 2019)

been much slower in SSA than in Asia and Latin America. The UN low variant projection (with fertility a half birth below the medium variant) estimates a population of 2.7 billion in 2100. This low variant could well be achieved with substantial new investments in family planning to meet a rising demand for contraception as desired family size declines. In that case, the population of SSA in 2100 would be nearly 2.5 billion lower than projected in the UN high variant and 1.1 billion below the medium variant. Clearly, a small reduction in fertility (1 birth per woman) has a large impact on future population growth (2.5 billion).

The alternative UN population projections also differ in their associated age distributions. Figure 7.15 plots the proportion of working age people for each projection variant in SSA. As expected, the high variant (with the highest fertility) has a much lower pace of increase in this proportion than the low variant. The peak of the dividend period occurs in the next few decades with the dividend about twice as large in the low than in the high variant.

The main conclusion from this exercise is that small differences in fertility trends can cause large differences in future demographic trends. Family planning programs can bring about fertility declines of about 1.5 births per woman; thus, they can potentially have a large impact on population size and age structure in future decades.

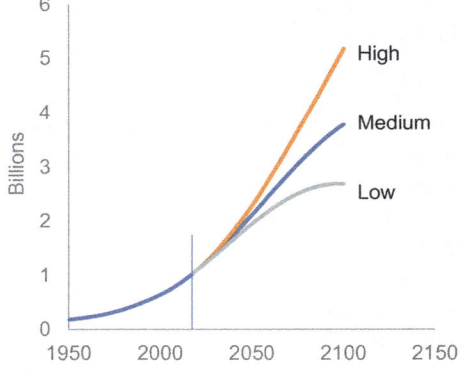

Fig. 7.14 Population projection variants, Sub-Saharan Africa (United Nations, 2019)

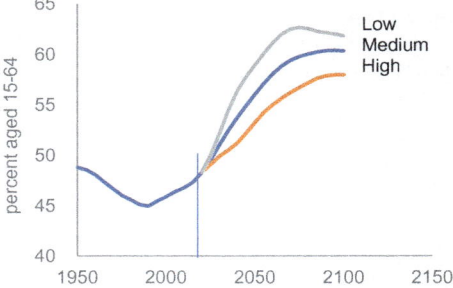

Fig. 7.15 Percent of population aged 18–64, Sub-Saharan Africa (United Nations, 2019)

7.6 Critics of Family Planning Programs

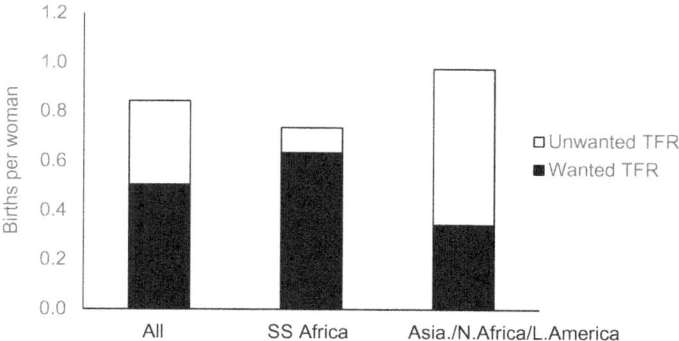

Fig. 7.16 Average decline in TFR, and its wanted and unwanted components between first and last DHS surveys after 1990 (Bongaarts, 2021)

7.6 Critics of Family Planning Programs

As discussed in Chap. 5, the literature on the fertility impact of family planning programs has been contentious. The most detailed and influential of these critiques was published in 1993 by Lant Pritchett. In contrast to earlier critiques (Davis, 1967; Demeny, 1979; Hauser, 1967) Pritchett undertook extensive analyses of reproductive statistics that had been gathered in World Fertility Survey and DHS up to about 1990.

To assess the separate roles of socio-economic development and family planning programs Pritchett examined the available empirical evidence on levels of wanted and unwanted fertility in a large number of developing countries. His main findings were that there is a strong—about one to one—correlation between wanted fertility (WTFR) and the TFR, but no significant correlation between unwanted fertility (UWTFR) and TFR. He drew several conclusions:

a) *"Excess" or "unwanted" fertility plays a minor role in explaining fertility* (Pritchett, 1994: 34)

This claim has been found problematic in several subsequent studies (Bongaarts, 1994, 1997, 2011, 2020; Casterline, 2009; Lam, 2011). The central flaw in Pritchett's analysis was its reliance on cross-sectional data because in the early 1990s relatively few countries had repeated fertility surveys. As the number of surveys has grown in the 1990s and 2000s an increasing number of countries have at least two surveys, thus allowing the estimation of actual changes over time in fertility indicators.

Figure 7.16 presents an updated decomposition of the change in the TFR into wanted and unwanted components.[3] The trends are derived by comparing fertility estimates from the earliest and latest available DHS surveys (on average from 1996 to 2014) in 54 countries from Bongaarts (2021).

Key findings:

---

[3] Wanted and unwanted fertility is estimated with a procedure proposed by Bongaarts (1990).

- The average decline in the TFR (0.84) for all countries substantially exceeds the decline in the wanted TFR (0.51). This finding is contrary to Pritchett expectation of approximately equal changes in the wanted TFR and total TFR. The same is true for the regional estimates.
- The average unwanted TFR for all countries declined by 0.34 (from 1.0 to 0.66), while Pritchett predicted constant unwanted fertility. The decline in the unwanted TFR accounts for 40% of the decline in the TFR in all countries. This is consistent with the findings of Casterline (2010), Lam (2011) and Günther and Harttgen (2016).
- Substantial differences exist between regions: the contribution of decline in the wanted TFR is much larger in Asia/N.Africa/L.America (65%) than in SS Africa (14%).

These findings demonstrate that the declines in unwanted fertility over time play an important role in reducing overall fertility.

b) *If improved family planning programs were driving fertility declines, they should be accompanied by a reduction in excess fertility. This is not the case* (Pritchett, 1994: 34).

This statement ignores the rise in the exposure to the risk of unwanted pregnancies that occurs as desired family size declines. As discussed in the previous section, in the absence of contraception, a decline in desired family size would be accompanied by a roughly equivalent rise in unwanted/excess births because women have three decades of potential reproductive years when they are usually sexually active and biologically capable of getting pregnant. In reality, such huge increases in unwanted fertility are not observed because women practice contraception, but unwanted births nevertheless occur because of the obstacles to contraceptive use and because of contraceptive failure. Family planning programs reduce but do not eliminate these obstacles. As a result, a substantial impact of family planning programs is consistent with a non-declining level of unwanted fertility in the early phases of the fertility transition.

c) In his discussion of the Matlab experiment Pritchett admits its large impact on contraceptive use and fertility, but then claims: "*The fertility changes were large not because fertility was particularly responsive to program intervention but because the effort was massive and expensive. This program expense makes it unlikely that this degree of effort will be replicated at a national scale in Bangladesh, or in any low-income country.*" (Pritchett, 1994: 36)

This statement is incorrect as demonstrated by the experience of Bangladesh and several other poor African countries such as Ethiopia, Malawi and Rwanda. Once the success of the Matlab project became known around 1980, the government of Bangladesh implemented a nationwide program based on the lessons from this experiment. As shown in Fig. 7.2 the country's modern contraceptive use rose rapidly and reached 27% in 1990 and 54% in 2015, well ahead of the mCPR in Pakistan. Another demonstration of the impact of the introduction of a nationwide family planning program is found in Iran. As documented in Chap. 2 Iran had the most rapid fertility decline in the developing world with the TFR declining from above 6 in 1986 to below 2.5 in 1997. Socio-economic indicators improved during this period, but not at an extraordinary rate. The most plausible main explanation for Iran's rapid fertility decline is the introduction of a family planning program around 1990 (Roudi-Fahimi, 2002).

> d) *fertility desires are largely determined by socio-economic forces other than family planning and .. fertility desires determine fertility* (Pritchett, 1994: 19). *In the conclusion:* "we have focused ..on the importance of desired fertility in explaining fertility variations and on the relatively small independent role of contraceptive access (or family planning programs more generally).* (Prichett, 1994: 41)

These statements reveal two common but erroneous assumptions made by Pritchett and other critics. First is the suggestion that family planning programs are only about access to contraceptive supplies. Earlier in this chapter we discussed the many other obstacles that face potential users of contraception and the key role family planning programs play in addressing these obstacles. Access is of course part of the reason for unplanned pregnancy, but family planning programs have much broader objectives. The second problem with the above statement is that Pritchett assumes that family planning programs have no effect on wanted fertility. As argued above, fertility preferences are affected by media campaigns implemented by programs and by statements from government officials. The evidence presented in the regression analyses summarized in Tables 7.1 and 7.2 document the important role of family planning programs as a determinant of demand for contraception and on wanted fertility (see also Bongaarts, 2011).

In short, Pritchett's influential analysis is seriously flawed. He correctly concluded that fertility preferences are a key driver of fertility declines. But his claims that unwanted fertility is nearly constant and that family planning programs have trivial effects are incorrect.

7.7 Conclusion

This chapter examined the long-standing debate about the extent to which family planning programs influence contraceptive behavior and fertility. Three sources of evidence were examined: (1) controlled experiments; (2) natural experiments; and (3) statistical analyses. The three sources provided broadly comparable estimates of the impact of a family planning program i.e., a rise of 25–35% in contraceptive prevalence and a decline of 1.5 births per woman in the TFR. The regression analysis was also used to examine the effects of family planning programs on contraceptive demand and its satisfaction, and on wanted and unwanted fertility. As expected, family planning programs increase the satisfaction of the demand for contraception and reduce unwanted fertility. Contrary to common assumptions made in economic theories of fertility, family planning programs also have a substantial impact on the demand for contraception and on wanted fertility. These findings help explain why family planning programs have been effective in several countries in SSA where desired family size has historically been high relative to other regions in the developing world.

References

Ahlburg, D., & Diamond, I. (1996). Evaluating the impact of family planning programs. In D. A. Ahlburg, A. C. Kelley & K. O. Mason (Eds.), *The impact of population growth on well-being in developing countries* (pp. 299–336). Springer.

Bongaarts, J. (1990). The measurement of wanted fertility. *Population and Development Review, 16*, 487–506.

Bongaarts, J. (1994). The impact of population policies: Comment [on Pritchett]. *Population and Development Review, 20*(3), 616–620.

Bongaarts, J. (1997). The role of family planning programmes in contemporary fertility transitions. In G. Jones, J. Caldwell, R. Douglas, & R. D'Souza (Eds.), *The continuing demographic transition* (pp. 422–444). Oxford University Press.

Bongaarts, J. (2011). Can family planning programs affect high desired family size in sub-Saharan Africa? *International Perspectives on Sexual and Reproductive Health, 37*(4), 209–216.

Bongaarts, J. (2020). Trends in fertility and fertility preferences in sub-Saharan Africa: The roles of education and family planning programs. *Genus, 76*, 32.

Bongaarts, J. (2021). The effects of family planning programs on wanted and unwanted fertility in sub-Saharan Africa. In *Paper presented at the session on population policies and the demographic transition at the 2021 IUSSP international population conference.*

Bongaarts, J., & Bruce, J. (1995). The causes of unmet need for contraception and the social content of services. *Studies in Family Planning, 26*(2), 57–75.

Bongaarts, J., Cleland, J., Townsend, J., Bertrand, J., Das Gupta, M. (2012). *Family planning programs for the 21st century: Rationale and design.* Population Council.

Bongaarts, J., & Hardee, K. (2017). The role of public-sector family planning programs in meeting the demand for contraception in sub-Saharan Africa. *International Perspectives on Sexual and Reproductive Health, 43*(2), 41–50.

Bongaarts, J., & Hardee, K. (2019). Trends in contraceptive prevalence in sub-Saharan Africa: The roles of family planning programs and education. *African Journal of Reproductive Health, 23*(3), 96–105.

Casterline, J. (2009). Demographic transition and unwanted fertility: A fresh assessment. *Pakistan Development Review, 48*(4), 387–421.

Casterline, J., Perez, A., & Biddlecom, A. (1997). Factors underlying unmet need for family planning in the Philippines. *Studies in Family Planning, 28*(3), 173–191.

Casterline, J., & Sinding, S. (2000). Unmet need for family planning in developing countries and implications for population policy. *Population and Development Review, 26*(4), 691–723.

Casterline, J., Sathar, Z., & Ul Haque, M. (2001). Obstacles to contraceptive use in Pakistan: A study in Punjab. *Studies in Family Planning, 32*(2), 95–110.

Cleland, J. (1994). Different pathways to demographic transition. In F. Graham-Smith (Ed.), *Population: The complex reality: A report of the Population Summit of the World's Scientific Academies* (pp. 229–247). Royal Society.

Cleland, J. (2001). Potatoes and pills: An overview of innovation-diffusion contributions to explanations of fertility decline. In J. B. Casterline (Ed.), *Diffusion processes and fertility transition: Selected perspectives* (pp. 39–65). National Academy Press.

Cleland, J. (forthcoming).. The contraceptive revolution In: J. May (Ed.), *International Handbook of Population Policies.* Springer.

Cleland, J., & Lush, L. (1997). Population and policies in Bangladesh, Pakistan. *Forum for Applied Research and Public Policy, 12*, 46–50.

Cleland, J., Bernstein, S., Ezeh, A., Faundes, A., Glasier, A., & Innis, J. (2006). Family planning: The unfinished agenda. *The Lancet, 368*(9549), 1810–1827.

Cleland, J., Phillips, J., Amin, S., & Kamal, G. (1994). The determinants of reproductive change in Bangladesh: Success in a challenging environment. Washington, DC: World Bank Group.

Curtis, S., & Neitzel, K. (1996). *Contraceptive knowledge, use, and sources.* DHS Comparative Studies No. 19: Macro International.

References

Davis, K. (1967). Population policy: Will current programs succeed? *Science, 158*, 730–739.

Demeny, P. (1979). On the end of the population explosion. *Population and Development Review, 5*(1), 141–162.

Debpuur, C., Phillips, J., Jackson, E., Nazzar, A., Ngom, P., & Binka, F. (2002). The impact of the Navrongo project on contraceptive knowledge and use, reproductive preferences, and fertility. *Studies in Family Planning, 33*(2), 141–164.

Donaldson, P. (1990). *Nature against us: The United States and the world population crisis, 1965–1980*. University of North Carolina Press.

El-Zanaty, F., Way, A., Kishor, S., & Casterline, J. (1999). *Egypt in-depth study on the reasons for nonuse of family planning*. National Population Council.

Fawcett, J. (1970). *Psychology and population*. The Population Council.

Feyisetan, B., & Casterline, J. (2000). Fertility preferences and contraceptive change in developing countries. *International Family Planning Perspectives, 26*(3), 100–109.

Foreit, J., & Frejka, T. (Eds.). (1998). *Family planning operations research: A book of readings*. Population Council.

Freedman, R., & Takeshita, J. (1969). *Family planning in Taiwan: An experiment in social change*. Princeton University Press.

Günther, I., & Harttgen, K. (2016). Desired fertility and number across time and space. *Demography, 53*, 55–83.

Hauser, P. (1967). Family planning and population: A book review article. *Demography, 4*(1), 397–414.

Hernandez, D. (1982). The impact of family planning programs on fertility in developing countries: A critical evaluation. *Journal of Social Research, 10*, 32–66.

ICDDR, B. (1994). Health and Demographic Surveillance System—Matlab, Volume 21, Registration of Health and Demographic Events 1992, Scientific Report No. 73, Health and Demographic Surveillance Unit, Public Health Sciences Division, International Centre for Diarrhoeal Disease Research, Dhaka, Bangladesh.

ICDDR, B. (2001). Health and Demographic Surveillance System—Matlab, Volume 32, Registration of Health and Demographic Events 1999, Scientific Report No. 88, Health and Demographic Surveillance Unit, Public Health Sciences Division, International Centre for Diarrhoeal Disease Research, Dhaka, Bangladesh.

ICF. (2021). The DHS Program STATcompiler. http://www.statcompiler.com. Retrieved September 29, 2021.

Kuang, B., & Brodsky, I. (2016). Global trends in family planning programs, 1999–2014. *International Perspectives on Sexual and Reproductive Health, 42*(1), 33–44.

Lam, D. (2011). How the world survived the population bomb: Lessons from 50 years of extraordinary demographic history. *Demography, 48*, 1231–1262.

Lee, K., Lush, L., Walt, G., & Cleland, J. (1998). Family planning policies and programmes in eight low-income countries: A comparative policy analysis. *Social Science in Medicine, 47*(7), 949–959.

Lightbourne, R. (1987). Reproductive preferences and behaviour. In J. Cleland & C. Scott (Eds.), *The world fertility survey: An assessment* (pp. 838–861). Oxford University Press.

Mauldin, W. (1965). Fertility studies: Knowledge, attitude, and practice. *Studies in Family Planning, 1*(7), 1–10.

Mauldin, W., & Ross, J. (1991). Family planning programs: Efforts and results, 1982–1989. *Studies in Family Planning, 22*(6), 350–367.

May, J. (2017). The politics of family planning policies and programs in sub-Saharan Africa. In: J. Casterline & J. Bongaarts (Eds.), *Fertility transition in sub-Saharan Africa, Population and Development Review 43*(Suppl.), 308–329.

Miller, G., & Babiarz, K. (2016). Family planning program effects: Evidence from microdata. *Population and Development Review, 42*(1), 7–26.

National Institute of Population Studies (NIPS) Pakistan and ICF. (2019). Pakistan demographic and health survey 2017–2018.

Phillips, J., Simmons, R., Koenig, M., & Chakraborty, J. (1988). The determinants of reproductive change in a traditional society: Evidence from Matlab Bangladesh. *Studies in Family Planning, 19*(6), 313–334.

Phillips, J., Stinson, W., Bhatia, S., Rahman, M., & Chakraborty, J. (1982). The demographic impact of the family planning-health services project in Matlab Bangladesh. *Studies in Family Planning, 13*(5), 131–140.

Piotrow, P. (1973). *World population crisis: The United States response.* Praeger.

Pritchett, L. (1994). Desired fertility and the impact of population policies. *Population and Development Review, 20*(1), 1–55.

Robinson, W., & Ross, J. A. (Eds.). (2007). *The global family planning revolution: Three decades of population policies and programs.* World Bank.

Ross, J., & Smith, E. (2011). Trends in national family planning programs, 1999, 2004 and 2009. *International Perspectives on Sexual and Reproductive Health, 37*(3), 125–133.

Roudi-Fahimi, F. (2002). *Iran's family planning program: Responding to a nation's needs.* Population Reference Bureau.

Tsui, A. (2001). Population policies, family planning programs, and fertility: The record. In: R. Bulatao, J. Casterline (eds.), Global fertility transition. *Population and Development Review 27*(Supplement), 184–204.

United Nations Population Division. (2019). World population prospects 2019, Online Edition. Rev.1. Department of Economic and Social Affairs, United Nations.

United Nations Population Division. (2021). Estimates and projections of family planning indicators 2021. United Nations.

Wittgenstein Centre for Demography and Global Human Capital. (2021). Wittgenstein Centre Data Explorer Version 1.2. http://www.wittgensteincentre.org/dataexplorer. Reterived May 3, 2021.

World Bank. (2021). World development indicators. World Bank Group. https://data.worldbank.org/indicator.

Open Access This chapter is licensed under the terms of the Creative Commons Attribution 4.0 International License (http://creativecommons.org/licenses/by/4.0/), which permits use, sharing, adaptation, distribution and reproduction in any medium or format, as long as you give appropriate credit to the original author(s) and the source, provide a link to the Creative Commons license and indicate if changes were made.

The images or other third party material in this chapter are included in the chapter's Creative Commons license, unless indicated otherwise in a credit line to the material. If material is not included in the chapter's Creative Commons license and your intended use is not permitted by statutory regulation or exceeds the permitted use, you will need to obtain permission directly from the copyright holder.

Chapter 8
The Developing World's Fertility Transition: 2000–2020

8.1 Introduction

In Chap. 1 we identified three phases in the developing world's aggregate fertility transition: a 1950–1970 pre-transition phase, a 1970–2000 rapid decline phase, and a 2000–2020 slow decline phase with low fertility. In the pre-transition phase, the developing world's fertility was high with an average TFR of about six throughout the period (Fig. 1.1); only a small number of developing countries began their fertility transitions prior to 1970 (Fig. 2.1). During the period from 1970 to 2000 most countries began their fertility transitions, with diverse starting times and transition trajectories (Fig. 2.4). After 2000 the countries of the developing world no longer possessed a common fertility trend or fertility level. In 2020 the TFRs of the 97 developing countries we examined in detail in Chap. 2 ranged from a high of 6.7 (Niger) to a low of 1.1 (South Korea), and the aggregate (weighted) TFR of all countries, 2.6, was only slightly lower than its turn-of-the-century level, 2.9. In the midst of this diversity, telling a single fertility story for the period 2000–2020 that encompasses all developing countries is impossible.

Dividing the 97 developing countries with population above 1 million[1] into three fertility groups based on their 2020 fertility levels permits a more accurate representation of the contemporary situation (Table 8.1). Country population sizes within each of the three fertility groups vary greatly. Since our focus is on understanding how conditions vary across the populations within the three fertility groups, all data for regions in this chapter will be weighted by population size. For example, when the 2020 TFR of the high fertility group is reported as 4.9 in Table 8.1, it is the average TFR of the entire population living in all high fertility countries. Since over 70% of the developing world's population now lives in low fertility countries, the "All 97 Countries" data tracks closely to the low fertility group's data.

---

[1] These 97 countries contain 6.33 billion people which amounts to 97% of the developing world's total population of 6.52 billion.

© The Author(s) 2022
J. Bongaarts and D. Hodgson, *Fertility Transition in the Developing World*,
SpringerBriefs in Population Studies,
https://doi.org/10.1007/978-3-031-11840-1_8

Table 8.1 Size and growth of three fertility groups, 2020

TFR level, 2020	Number of countries	Population size 2020 (million)	Average TFR 2020	Rate of pop growth 2015–2020	Percent pop of Dev world	Percent pop of world
Low: below 2.5	42	4,676	2.0	0.9	72	60
Middle: 2.5–4.0	26	702	3.3	2.0	11	9
High: above 4.0	29	953	4.9	2.8	15	12
Total	97	6,331	2.6	1.3	97	81

Sources TFR, UN: POP/DB/WPP/Rev.2019/INT/F01
Population Size, UN: POP/DB/WPP/Rev.2019/SA1/POP/F01-1
Annual Population Growth Rate, 2015–2020, UN: POP/DB/WPP/Rev.2019/SA1/POP/F03

The "low" fertility group consists of 42 countries with TFRs below 2.5; all have completed their fertility transitions. This low fertility population has a 2020 TFR of 2.0 and an annual population growth rate below 0.9%. The "middle" fertility group consists of 26 countries with TFRs between 2.5 and 4 that have made substantial progress traversing their fertility transition. This middle fertility population has a TFR of 3.3 and an annual population growth rate of 2%. The "high" fertility group consists of 29 countries with TFRs greater than 4 that have experienced limited fertility declines from pre-transition levels. The high fertility population has a TFR of 4.9 and a high annual population growth rate of 2.8%. The UN projects that its 2020 population of 953 million will double to 1.9 billion by 2050. The appendix in Chap. 2 lists the countries in each group. These "low," "middle," and "high" fertility groups have very different demographic, geographic, socio-economic, health, and educational characteristics. They also face very different fertility and development challenges. Some have the lowest below-replacement fertility levels ever recorded (Taiwan, South Korea), and desire to increase their fertility, others have very high fertility (Niger, Mali), and seek to lower their fertility. The particular challenges facing each group will be treated separately.

Currently 4.7 billion of the developing world's population have completed their fertility transitions; they represent 72% of the developing world's population, and 60% of the world's population (Table 8.1). The controversies surrounding population control efforts recounted in Chap. 5 have receded as more countries completed their transitions. When many governments perceived rapid population growth to be a significant problem, some implemented antinatalist policies that pressured women to have fewer children than they desired. At the 1994 United Nations Cairo Conference on Population and Development reproductive rights advocates helped to fashion a Program of Action that proscribed the use of incentives, disincentives and quotas to limit births. As a result, high pressure or coercive antinatalist programs are no longer a major threat to women's reproductive health or rights. For example, after reaching below replacement fertility, China recently ended what had been the most egregious coercive anti-natalist program, its one-child program. Attention is still needed in China and elsewhere because of the possible future threat of coercive pronatalist programs in response to continued very low, below replacement fertility, population aging and eventual population decline. In contrast, women in the high fertility group (mostly in Africa) face a very different challenges to their reproductive health and rights, ranging from child marriages to high maternal mortality. They also have a significant unmet need for contraception, and unplanned pregnancies and abortion remain common (Fig. 3.6). Each set of challenges will be addressed separately.

8.2 Characteristics of the Three Fertility Groups

Demographic and health differences among the three fertility groups are significant and consistently document the more challenging conditions experienced by high fertility populations (Table 8.2). Some of these contrasting conditions flow directly from fertility differences. For example, in the high fertility group of countries the median age of the population is low because each woman on average gives birth to four or more children. With such high fertility, the younger generation always will be significantly larger that the parental generation, often half the population will be under 18, and parents will be tasked with the care of many children. In contrast, in the low fertility population with a TFR of 2.0, mothers have just two children each, resulting in a higher median age. The connection between fertility decline and a rising median age are evident in the case of China, whose fertility transition from high to low is shown on Fig. 1.2. In the decade of the 1960s China's TFR was 6.3, by 1980–1985 it fell to 2.5, by 1990–1995 it fell to 1.6, where it has remained. China's median age was 19.3 in 1970 and rose steadily to 38.4 in 2020. As China's fertility went from high to low, changes in its median age mirror those found on Table 8.2 among the three fertility groups.

China's fertility decline also illustrates the dynamic that produces change in the total dependency ratio. This ratio is defined as the number of dependent-aged persons (aged 0 to 14 and 65 and older) that 100 active-aged persons (aged 15 to 64) support. The 1960–1970 birth cohort, born when the TFR was 6.3, was China's last relatively large birth cohort. In 1970 the total dependency ratio was 79.1. As the relatively smaller 1970–1980 birth cohort replaced that large cohort with the new 0–10 population during the 1970s, China's total dependency ratio fell to 68.4 by 1980. Additional smaller birth cohorts entered the population over the next decades leading the total dependency ratio to fall to 52.0 in 1990, 46.2 in 2000, and 36.5 in 2010, but then in 2020 it increased to 42.2. By 2020 the 1960–1970 birth cohort, China's last relatively large cohort, was aged 50 to 60. Over the next decade it will join the survivors of other older large cohorts in the dependent-aged 65 and older group. As the small cohorts generated from declining fertility enter the ranks of the 15 to 64 population, the total dependency ratio can expect to continue to increase, especially since China's fertility has remained well below replacement level. A stable TFR of 1.6 will continually produce offspring who are fewer in number than their parents.

Table 8.2 Demographic and health characteristics of three fertility groups

TFR lvel 2020	Median age 2020	Total dependency ratio, 2020	Life expectancy at birth, 2019	Infant mortality rate, 2018	Maternal mortality ratio, 2017
Low: below 2.5	32.4	46.2	73.7	17.7	85.7
Middle: 2.5–4.0	22.9	65.6	69.0	36.3	153.2
High: above 4.0	18.0	86.3	60.9	55.4	574.0
All 97 Countries: (Weighted TFR: 2.56)	29.2	54.3	71.3	25.2	163.6

Sources TFR, UN: POP/DB/WPP/Rev.2019/INT/F01
Median Age, UN: POP/DB/WPP/Rev.2019/SA1/POP/F05
Total Dependency Rate, UN: POP/DB/WPP/Rev.2019/SA1/POP/F11-A
Life Expectancy and Infant Mortality Rate, UN: POP/DB/WPP/Rev.2019/INT/F01
Maternal Mortality: www.who.int/reproductivehealth/publications/maternal-mortality-2000-2017

The UN (2019) projects that by 2060 China's total dependency ratio again will be in the high 70s, about its 1970 level. Its dependent population in 2060, however, will be composed of many more older than younger individuals.

China's 1970–2020 total dependency ratio changes mirror those found on Table 8.2 among the three fertility groups. It also illustrates several points that were made in Chap. 5. At present, the low fertility population (Table 8.2) is still in the middle of its first demographic dividend: 100 active-aged 15- to 64-year-olds only need to provide for 46 dependent-aged individuals. This contrasts with 100 active-aged individuals in the high fertility population needing to provide for 86 dependent-aged individuals, a much greater burden for a population with significantly fewer resources (Table 8.3). China's experience has lessons for both populations. The high fertility population can observe the benefits that accompany lower fertility and a decline in its dependency burden. The lesson for the low fertility population concerns the temporary nature of the first demographic dividend. The present is the time for its active-aged individuals to save and accumulate assets to help provide for their old age. Today's action, or inaction, will determine the size and longevity of its second demographic dividend.

The three measures of health in Table 8.2—life expectancy, infant mortality, and maternal mortality—all are highly correlated with a population's fertility level. The maternal mortality ratio, maternal deaths per 100,000 live births, clearly illustrates this relationship. It is nearly seven times higher for the high fertility population (574) than for the low fertility one (85.7) largely because of the different resources of the two population. Maternal deaths generally result from severe bleeding after childbirth, infections, untreated high blood pressure during pregnancy, and complications from delivery. It can be significantly reduced by high quality care in pregnancy, and during and after childbirth. Each of these, however, requires resources that are scarce in

8.2 Characteristics of the Three Fertility Groups

Table 8.3 Socio-economic characteristics of three fertility groups

TFR level, 2020	GNI per capita Atlas Method, 2020	Percent employed in agriculture, 2019	Percent urban 2019	Mean years of schooling, 2019	HDI 2019
Low: below 2.5	$6,529	29.4	53.6	7.8	0.719
Middle: 2.5–4.0	$2,274	33.4	44.8	6.4	0.613
High: above 4.0	$1,152	53.1	38.9	5.0	0.503
All 97 Countries: (Weighted TFR: 2.56)	$5,248	33.3	50.4	7.2	0.675

Sources TFR, UN: POP/DB/WPP/Rev.2019/INT/F01
GNI per capita, Atlas method (current US$): https://data.worldbank.org/indicator/NY.GNP.PCAP.PP.CD
Percent Employed in Agriculture: ILO (2020). ILOSTAT database https://ilostat.ilo.org/data/
Percent Urban: World Urbanization Prospects: The 2018 Revision. New York. https://esa.un.org/unpd/wup/
Mean Years of Schooling: UNESCO Institute for Statistics (2020), Barro and Lee (2018), ICF Macro Demographic and Health Surveys, UNICEF Multiple Indicator Cluster Surveys and OECD (2019)
HDI: HDRO calculations based on data from UNDESA (2019), UNESCO Institute for Statistics (2020), United Nations Statistics Division (2020), World Bank (2020), Barro and Lee (2018) and IMF (2020)

countries with low incomes and are difficult to provide to more rural populations. The infant mortality rate, deaths to infants under one per 1,000 births, is a little more than three times as high in the high fertility population (55.4) than in the low fertility population (17.7). In sub-Saharan Africa, the home of most of the world's high fertility population, the IMR was 107.6 as recently as 1990, but has since declined to 52.5 as efforts to strengthen a range of public health measures continue. Life expectancy in sub-Saharan Africa, which stagnated at 50 during the decade of the 1990s as HIV infections spread, has since increased to 61.5 as antiretroviral treatment became more available and as infant mortality declined. It still, however, is nearly 13 years shorter than that of the low fertility population.

The correlation, across multiple dimensions, between low fertility and different indicators of development is evident in Table 8.3. Compared to the developing world's high fertility population, its low fertility population has a five and one-half times greater per capita income, 56% more schooling, lower rates of agricultural employment, and higher rates of urban residence. Its Human Development Index (HDI), a composite development measure based on life expectancy, income, and schooling, is 43% higher. These differences are reminiscent of those existing between the developed world and the developing world at mid-twentieth century. At that time the entire developing world was the high fertility group (TFR of 6.2), and the developed world was the low fertility population (TFR of 2.8). The contrasting development indicators back then were dramatic: life expectancy of 40.5 versus 63.4, infant mortality rate of 164.5 versus 66.7, percent living in cities of 54.8% versus 17.7%. What is just as dramatic, however, is how far the low fertility portion of the developing world's population has come over the last seventy years. It now has a TFR of 2, a life expectancy of 73.7, an infant mortality rate of 17.7, a Gross National Income of $6,529 per capita in current US$, and an average of nearly 8 years of schooling. Its life expectancy is 16% higher than the developed world's 1950 life expectancy, and its infant mortality is 73% lower.

The fact that 72% of the developing world's population was able to complete their fertility transition and attain such significant development advances does provide the remaining 28% of the developing world with an achievable goal. In the mid-twentieth century, debates raged over whether substantial fertility declines and development were attainable goals for the world's "less developed regions" (Chap. 5). There is no such debate now concerning the potential for advancement of the middle and high fertility populations. The evidence reviewed in Chap. 4 indicates that some of the correlations between development indicators and fertility are not causal. In particular, GDP per capita and urbanization have little or no impact on reproductive behavior. Instead, improvements in the education of women, child survival and family planning programs have been the main drivers of fertility transitions. This is welcome news for contemporary poor countries because large increases in GDP per capita are difficult to realize quickly, while improvements in human development can be achieved in relatively short period of time and at lower costs. Poor countries that have emphasized investments in education, public health and family planning programs have seen rapid declines in fertility and benefited from the demographic dividend.

8.3 Characteristics of Geographic Groups

The high fertility group (TFR > 4) has the closest association with a particular geographic region. Twenty-seven of the 29 countries in that fertility group are located in West, Middle, and East Africa, including every country in the Sahel (see appendix to Chap. 2). The two additional high fertility countries are Sudan, which technically is a North African country, and Afghanistan. There are six additional West, Middle, and East African countries that are in the middle fertility group (Madagascar, Eritrea, Rwanda, Ghana, Zimbabwe, and Kenya), but four of them have TFRs that are very close to 4. So, there is a remarkable overlap between the high fertility population and the West, Middle, and East African countries. Both are about 1 billion people in size with nearly identical TFRs (4.9 vs. 4.8). The demographic and socioeconomic characteristics of the "high fertility group" in Tables 8.2 and 8.3 are all similar to those of the West, Middle, East Africa region on Tables 8.4 and 8.5. In 2020 "high fertility" has a very specific geographic locus.

8.3 Characteristics of Geographic Groups

Table 8.4 Demographic characteristics of geographic groups

Geographic area	Pop 2020 (millions)	TFR 2020	Rate of pop growth 2015–2020	Total dependency ratio, 2020	Life expectancy 2019	Infant mortality rate, 2018
Africa: all	1,327	4.4	2.5	79.3	63.6	46.1
Africa: W, M, E	1,015	4.8	2.7	84.9	61.3	53.0
Africa: N, S	312	3.0	1.8	60.9	70.8	24.0
Asia	4,431	2.1	1.0	47.6	73.1	20.5
LA & Caribbean	564	2.0	1.1	48.7	75.5	14.4
All 96 Countries:	6,322	2.6	1.29	54.3	71.3	25.2

Note Data for Papua New Guinea, a developing country in Oceania, is not included in this table
Population Size, UN: POP/DB/WPP/Rev.2019/SA1/POP/F01-1
Annual Population Growth Rate, 2015–2020, UN: POP/DB/WPP/Rev.2019/SA1/POP/F03
Other Data: See Table 8.3 sources

Table 8.5 Socio-economic characteristics of geographic groups

Geographic area	GNI per capita Atlas method 2020	Percent employed in agriculture, 2019	Percent urban, 2019	Mean years of schooling, 2019	HDI 2019
Africa: all	$1,762	46.2	42.9	5.8	0.554
Africa: W, M, E	$1,258	54.0	39.2	5.3	0.514
Africa: N, S	$3,401	21.2	55.0	7.3	0.683
Asia	$6,088	31.8	49.0	7.5	0.701
LA & Caribbean	$6,892	14.7	79.9	8.4	0.756
All 96 Countries:	$5,252	33.3	50.5	7.2	0.675

Note Data for Papua New Guinea, a developing country in Oceania, is not included in this table
Data See Table 8.4 sources

The middle fertility group (TFR 2.5–4.0) and the low fertility group (TFR < 2.5) contain countries from a mix of regions. Four North and Southern African countries are in the middle fertility group (Namibia, Egypt, Lesotho, and Algeria) and five are in the low fertility group (Morocco, Libya, Tunisia, South Africa and Mauritius). On Tables 8.4 and 8.5 African data are presented separately for West, Middle, and East Africa and for North and Southern Africa because these two regions have distinct demographic and socio-economic patterns. Most large Asian and Latin American countries are among the 42 countries in the low fertility group. With 70% of the developing world's population living in Asia, the data for "All 96 Countries" closely tracks Asian trends; and with 76% of Africa's population living in West, Middle, and East Africa, that region closely tracks "Africa: all" trends. Data from Papua New Guinea, the sole country from Oceania, is not included in Tables 8.4 and 8.5.

West, Middle, and East Africa, with over one billion people, has made noticeably less headway traversing the fertility transition than other geographic regions. Its TFR of 4.8 is 1.8 births higher than that of North and Southern Africa, and 2.8 births higher than that of Asia and Latin America. Its health conditions are also noticeably poorer. Life expectancy is 9.5 years lower than in North and Southern Africa, 11.8 years lower than in Asia, and 14.2 years lower than Latin America. Its infant mortality rate is about four times that of Latin America, two and one-half times that of Asia and more than twice that of North and Southern Africa. Its dependency burden is substantially higher: one hundred 15- to 64-year-olds need to provide for 85 dependent-aged persons, compared to 48 in Asia and Latin America. Its very high annual population growth rate (2.74%) implies a short population doubling time; the UN projects that by 2050 its population will double to over two billion. Its first demographic dividend will be limited in the near future unless there is a sizable fertility decline soon.

Unsurprisingly, the West, Middle, East Africa region has notable poor socio-economic conditions (Table 8.5). Its per capita Gross National Income is 37% that of North and Southern Africa, 21% that of Asia, and 18% that of Latin America. Most of its workforce still is employed in the agricultural sector and less than 40% of the population resides in cities. Its population has two years fewer schooling than that of North and Southern Africa, 2.2 years fewer than that of Asia, and 3.1 years fewer than that of Latin America. The United Nations Development Programme places its Human Development Index (0.514) in the "low human development" category while that of North and Southern Africa and of Asia is in the "medium human development" category, and that of Latin America is in the "high human development" category. The Latin America and Caribbean region has somewhat better socio-economic and health characteristics than Asia, although it has similar fertility, population growth, and dependency measures.

Understanding the challenges faced by the world's 2020 high fertility population requires an understanding of the relationship between fertility and development in West, Middle, and East Africa, a relationship that has been affected by the region's history, culture, politics, economics and physical environment. The challenges faced by the developing world's middle fertility population and its low fertility population, both widely dispersed among countries in different geographic areas, are less likely to flow from a particular region and are more likely to be related to a particular stage in the transition process.

8.4 The Challenges Facing the Developing World's High Fertility Population

When examining the fertility transition of geographic regions in Chap. 2, we noted (Table 2.1) something unusual about the experience of sub-Saharan African countries. Their transition started later than those of Asian and Latin American countries

(1990 vs. 1972), their pre-transition fertility was higher (7.1 vs. 6.8), in the first decade of their transitions their rate of fertility decline was slower (13% vs. 23%), and their 2020 TFR level was higher (4.4 vs. 2.3). We labeled this the "Africa effect." Bongaarts (2017) analyzed the association between fertility decline and a variety of measures of development (GDP per capita, schooling, life expectancy, and urbanization) and uncovered possible reasons for these effects. Unlike in Asia and Latin America, in sub-Saharan Africa GDP per capita temporarily slumped in the 1980s and 1990s, not rising above the 1970 level until after 2000. Likewise, instead of experiencing a normal continuous rise in life expectancy, the AIDS pandemic struck sub-Saharan Africa especially hard, and life expectancy stalled at 50 from the mid-1980s through the 1990s. These stalls likely delayed the onset of its fertility transition. Once it started, the pace of improvement in development indicators was relatively slow, as was the rate of fertility decline. These "Africa effects," therefore, had conventional developmental roots. Bongaarts also uncovered one unique effect: at a given level of development, sub-Saharan fertility was higher, its desired family size was higher, and its contraceptive use was lower. This cluster of differences suggests elements in sub-Saharan Africa's culture and social structure that foster high fertility.

The above analysis looks at sub-Saharan Africa, a grouping that includes the more advanced countries of Southern Africa. The high fertility population (2020 TFR > 4) described in Tables 8.2 and 8.3 is a subset of this population that includes only the 27 highest fertility countries of West, Middle, and East Africa along with Sudan and Afghanistan. And all the "Africa effects" described above are heightened within this subgroup. In Fig. 2.1 the 1950–2020 fertility trends of these 29 countries appear as red lines. Their fertility transitions began later than 1990, their fertility declines were slower than in "middle fertility" countries (blue lines), and much slower than in "low fertility" countries (green lines). In fact, between 1950 and 2000 there was very little change in the high fertility population's TFR, just a 2.6% decline from 6.6 to 6.3, while its population increased 3.5-fold from 153 to 539 million. This half-century of near constant fertility coexisted with some significant socioeconomic and health changes: urbanization increased from 8% in 1950 to 29% in 2000, life expectancy increased from 34 to 50 years, and infant mortality fell from 195 to 99.

That these non-trivial changes had so little effect on fertility suggests that cultural and social structural factors common to West, Middle, and East African societies were fostering high fertility (Caldwell et al., 1992: 214–215): a religion that stressed the importance of ancestry and descent; a family system in which the father made reproductive decisions but the mother and her dependent children bore the childrearing costs; and a communal land tenure system in which large families could demand a greater share of the land. Some data on schooling and adolescent fertility illustrates how these factors might influence fertility. There is male and female schooling data for twenty of the high fertility countries for the year 2000: males averaged 3.8 years of school and females 2.0 years. The overall low level of schooling and 47% sex differential indicate that few girls were attending school long enough to achieve literacy. The age-specific birth rate for ages 15–19 in 2000 was 139.5, meaning that about 70% of girls were likely to give birth before reaching age 20. Early female entry into partnerships and childbearing in a largely agricultural setting is a traditional start to very large families.

The high fertility population did begin its fertility transition in the mid-1990s, with its fertility falling from 6.3 to 4.9 by 2020, ending with a half-birth greater TFR than that of all sub-Saharan Africa (4.4). Although there currently is a low baseline of development with respect to GNI per capita, life expectancy, urbanization, and schooling (Tables 8.2 and 8.3), significant change did occur between 2000 and 2020: urbanization went from 29 to 39%, life expectancy added 11.5 years to 61.3, infant mortality was cut in half again to 49.9, males added two years to their schooling (6.1 years) as did females (4.0 years), adolescent fertility fell from 139.5 to 102.8, and several countries implemented family planning programs. These changes were accompanied by a 1.4 birth decline in TFR. The major challenge facing the high fertility group is how to invest further in education, health and family planning programs so that this population of 953 million can steadily move out of poverty and enhance its health. Currently their high fertility is slowing their development, and their poor health and low socio-economic conditions are thwarting persistent fertility decline.

Progress will not come easily. The World Bank estimates that West and Middle Africa experienced a decline in real GDP of 0.8% during the Covid induced recession of 2020, and predicts a rebound in real GDP of 3.2% in 2021 and 3.6% in 2022 (Zeufack et al., 2021: 36). But since the population growth rate of this region is 2.7%, the real GDP per capita actually declined by 3.5% in 2020, and is projected to experience a very modest rebound of 0.5% in 2021 and 0.9% in 2022, making up only half the GDP per capita lost in 2020. High fertility and rapid population growth magnify the economic impact of a downturn and dampen the economic benefits of an upturn. Climate change, although a global phenomenon, is having a particularly powerful effect on the high fertility population. Every country in the Sahel is a member of the high fertility population, and every Sahel country has recently experienced an increase in the number and severity of droughts. The World Bank (Zeufack et al., 2021: 69, 51) finds that one in four households in the Sahel "is vulnerable to repeated climate shocks" that contribute to maternal and child malnutrition, trigger school dropout, and induce poor households to sell productive assets. They also find that deforestation, non-sustainable agriculture, and overgrazing are challenging the livelihoods of farmers and herders throughout the region, leading to an increase in "civil conflict and political stability" as farming and herding ethnic groups fight over access to land for their still burgeoning populations.

In time, living conditions are likely to alter in ways that will highlight the benefits of a smaller family. The UN projects that by 2050 57% of the high fertility population will live in cities. In an urban environment the requirements for starting a family are likely to become more challenging for larger numbers of young people, and parents are likely to view education in a new light for both their sons and daughters. Schooling, not early partnerships and childbearing, will be the key to security and to lower fertility and desired family size. But about 60% of high fertility countries are "non-resource rich" countries according to the World Bank (Zeufack et al., 2021: 60), without appreciable amounts of oil, minerals, or metals to trade on world markets.

This set of countries might need significant international developmental aid to acquire the basic infrastructure needed for a viable non-agricultural economy.

Given the low levels of development that prevail in the high fertility population it is urgent that governments reduce the obstacles created by adverse demographic conditions, in particular high fertility, rapid population growth and high dependency ratio. Some policy makers believe that nothing can be done about these trends, because desired family size is high. This view ignores the clear evidence that voluntary family planning programs have been successful in a number of poor countries where governments have made a significant investment (e.g., Rwanda, Malawi and Ethiopia). This success is in part due the existence of high unmet need for spacing births. In addition, high desired family size has consistently declined after the introduction of well-designed family planning programs. As summarized in the preceding chapter, family planning programs and their information, education, and communication efforts can lead to a decline in desired family size that is independent of development. Increasing contraceptive use and declining fertility bring about a range of socio-economic benefits which make voluntary family planning programs a highly cost-effective development intervention.

8.5 The Challenges Facing the Developing World's Middle Fertility Population

The middle fertility population (2020 TFR 2.5–4) is geographically dispersed, comprised of populations from eleven Asian countries, eleven African countries, three Latin American and Caribbean countries, and Papua New Guinea. A variety of regions within each continent are represented, and the twenty-six countries share few common historical or cultural characteristics. The blue lines on Fig. 2.1 trace their 1950–2020 fertility trends. Their 1950 TFRs ranged from the lowest to the highest among all developing countries, and as a population their fertility transition began in 1980. Countries starting from pretransition fertility levels above 8 (Yemen, Rwanda, Oman) had especially steep early declines. Three countries (Laos, Jordan and Bolivia) now are close to completing their transitions.

Currently the weighted mean TFR of this population of 702 million is 3.3, significantly lower than the 4.9 mean for the high fertility population. Their health and socio-economic measures are also better (Tables 8.2 and 8.3), but their GNI per capita is just $1,122 greater than that of the high fertility population. This implies that large health and general development gains, and a significant drop in fertility, is associated with a relatively modest difference in GNI per capita. This is consistent with the finding of Chap. 4 that GNI per capita is not a statistically significant determinant of fertility decline. A possible reason for this population's more favorable current situation is that it started its fertility transition fifteen years earlier than the high fertility population (1980 vs. 1995). Although in 1950 both middle and high fertility populations had relatively similar life expectancies (38 vs. 34), infant mortality rates

(234 vs 195), and total fertility rates (6.8 vs. 6.6), by the year 2000 these rates had diverged significantly: the middle fertility population had a considerably higher life expectancy (63 vs. 50), lower infant mortality rate (61 vs. 99), and lower total fertility rate (4.5 vs. 6.3). Tables 8.2 and 8.3 document that significant differences in health, development, and demographic characteristics persist today. "Africa effects" also might be playing a role in these differences.

Another important trend is the increase in contraceptive use which is the key driver of fertility decline and the related demographic dividend. Contraceptive use among women in union rose sharply between 2000 and 2020 in both the high fertility population (from 14 to 27%) and in the middle fertility population (from 37 to 49%). These trends are caused by development changes (in particular girl's education and health) and by the expansion of family planning programs. The latter benefitted greatly from international commitments made at the 2012 London Summit on Family Planning FP2020. This global initiative was established in 2012 with the ambitious goal of adding by 2020 120 million users of modern contraceptives to the existing 260 million users in 69 priority countries. Over those eight years, ten developed countries annually contributed about $1.3 billion in bilateral aid to the effort (Scoggins & Bremner, 2021: 40–41). By 2020 an additional 60 million users of modern contraceptives were recorded. While this increase fell well short of the FP2020 goal, it represents about 12 million more users than would have been predicted on the basis of historical rates of growth in contraceptive use in place before the initiative (Stover & Sonneveldt, 2017: 84). A continuation of the initiative, FP2030, is now underway. Both initiatives are indicative of the enhanced priority that the international community has placed on voluntary family planning programs. This is a significant contrast to the fall-off in interest evident at last century's end. Having high quality family planning programs can significantly facilitate fertility decline, especially when desired family size declines (Chap. 7).

The middle fertility population faces several development challenges. As a population, it is forty-years into an ongoing fertility transition. Its TFR is 3.3, but still about 24% of women of reproductive age who want to stop or delay childbearing are not using a modern method of contraception (United Nations, 2022). Many pregnancies are unwanted or mistimed, and a significant percentage of these are aborted (Fig. 3.9). The on-going challenge for women in the middle fertility population is to learn how to integrate modern contraceptives into the new fertility regime they are adopting. As schooling is becoming more important, establishing partnerships and childbearing are being postponed to later ages and the desired number of children is falling to lower levels. In this new regime women find themselves with an increasing number of years in which they are fecund and sexually active but wanting no additional children. Learning how best to accomplish this new goal will be a continuing challenge, one that can be helped by high quality family planning programs (Chap. 7).

This population also has a major development goal that is related to its stage in the fertility transition: making full use of the economic benefits that come from its falling dependency ratio. When its fertility transition began around 1980, its total dependency ratio had peaked at 94, an 18% rise from its 1950 level of 80. With infant and child mortality declining from 1950 to 1980 while fertility remained at pre-transition levels, the proportion of the population below the age of 15 increased. With its fertility transition underway after 1980, the total dependency ratio began to decline as the proportion young declined. By 2000 it had fallen to 82, and by 2020 to 66. This population is now experiencing its first demographic dividend. With a high and growing percentage of its population in the active-ages, a significant boost to economic growth will result so long as productive work is readily available (Chap. 6). The UN projects that over the next thirty years the total dependency ratio will decline still further to 53. The challenge for the middle fertility population over this period will be to save more, and use those assets to enhance both human and physical capital. Investing in more schooling and better training will not only raise productivity, but it will also raise the age of household formation and further lower desired family size. If this challenge can be met, a substantial second demographic dividend will be ensured along with sustained prosperity (Chap. 6).

8.6 The Challenges Facing the Developing World's Low Fertility Population

The developing world's low fertility population did not exist until 1974 when Singapore's TFR fell below 2.5. In 1950 all of the 97 developing countries had TFRs well above 5; Singapore's was 6.5. It entered into its fertility transition in 1958 when its TFR fell 5% below its peak level, and completed its transition in 1974 (Fig. 2.4). That year the developing world's entire low fertility population consisted of Singapore's 2.2 million individuals. Taiwan joined the group in 1980, South Korea in 1981, Mauritius in 1982, Thailand in 1986, and China in 1989. In fifteen years, the low fertility population had expanded from 2.2 million to 1.3 billion, 31% of the developing world's population. Since then, 36 additional countries have completed their fertility transitions: 8 in the 1990s, 13 in the 2000s, and 15 in the 2010s. By 2020 the low fertility population reached 4.7 billion, 72% of the developing world's population.

Chronicling the growth in size and proportion of the low fertility population is an efficient way of summarizing the developing world's fertility transition. It also highlights several distinctive characteristics of this transition. It has largely been a one-way fertility trend: downward. Only two countries (Algeria and Mongolia) have ever exited the low fertility population. They both had TFRs that had fallen below 2.5 in the early years of this century, and then fertility increased enough to move back across the 2.5 line. In Chap. 2 we noticed a similar phenomenon in seven sub-Saharan African countries whose downward fertility trends appeared to have "stalled." Since none of the other thirty-five sub-Saharan countries had "stalled" transitions, we considered this an anomaly in need of further examination. Our response reflects our conviction that general development and fertility decline are integrally connected, that if health conditions and general socioeconomic conditions such as the education of women improve, then fertility should fall, especially if voluntary family planning programs are implemented. To date, this has largely been true. Eighty-five of the 97 countries examined had their lowest ever TFR in 2020, and it coincided with substantially improved health, socio-economic conditions and investments in family planning programs. That is not to say that countries with relatively modest levels of economic development cannot enter the low fertility group. They have already. Nepal, Cambodia, India, Bangladesh, and Honduras have GNIs per capita ranging from $1,200 to $2,200 and TFRs below 2.5. The most likely explanation for their low levels of fertility are investments in female education, public health and family planning programs (see Chaps. 4 and 7). This finding provides hope for poor countries in Africa that fertility decline and its many benefits can be achieved relatively soon.

But fertility transitions can come to end, and when that happens past relationships can change. Not one of the original formulators of transition theory (Chap. 5) predicted the post-WWII baby boom. Their firm belief that fertility decline was a consequence of "modernization," prevented them from envisioning fully modern societies experiencing significant increases in fertility. While there is little evidence of an imminent fertility increase in the developing world, an increasing number of countries have adopted pronatalist policies. The last UN survey of fertility policies was in 2015, and eleven of the 97 countries stated a desire to "raise" their fertility level. These eleven countries had a 2020 TFR of 1.7 and a population of 1.7 billion. As their fertility level declined to low levels, six countries (China, Iran, Mauritius, South Korea, Thailand, and Turkey) sequenced through all the fertility policies options on the UN policy surveys, first adopting a policy to "lower" fertility, then to "maintain" it, and finally to "raise" it. This trend of low fertility countries ending their transitions with below replacement fertility and a pronatalist policy position is likely to continue. Singapore has had a policy to "raise" fertility since 1996 when its TFR fell to 1.6. Countries with the lowest fertility tend to be both pronatalist and highly developed. Singapore, Taiwan, and South Korea all have a GNI per capita of over $30,000 and a TFR of 1.2 or less. There are pronatalist developing countries with somewhat higher TFRs and less exceptional levels of development. Thailand, China, and Turkey have GNIs of between $7,000 and $10,500, and TFRs between 1.5 and 2.0.

The countries that began their fertility transition in the late 1950 and 1960s and completed it by the late 1980s will face, over the next three decades, the challenge of rapidly aging populations. All had very rapid fertility transitions, twenty years or less in duration, and have already experienced several decades of well-below replacement level fertility. The UN projects that their median ages will increase considerably from 2020 to 2050: Singapore from 42.2 to 53.4, Taiwan from 42.5 to 54.2, South Korea from 43.7 to 56.5, Mauritius from 37.5 to 47.7, Thailand from 40.1 to 49.7, and China from 38.4 to 47.6. Their first demographic dividends will all end as their populations rapidly age and their total dependency ratios will increase. Implementing effective pronatalist programs is likely to become an important political priority for an increasing number of low fertility countries. The rapidity of aging is directly related to the rapidity of a country's fertility decline, and historically unprecedented rapid aging is an inevitable part of many low fertility countries' futures. Iran's entire fertility transition took just eleven years. Its TFR went from above 6 in 1986 to below 2.5 in 1997; extremely rapid aging will be a certainty for Iran in the first half of the twenty-first century.

The challenge for these countries will be to implement pronatalist policies that respect women's reproductive rights and preserve their reproductive health. Since the "problematic" low fertility is commonly accepted to be an expression of the actual fertility desires of women, given their social and economic circumstances, there is great potential for direct conflict between state goals and women's goals. States can induce higher fertility while still respecting the reproductive rights of women, but doing so without coercion requires an authentic state commitment to reproductive rights as well as significant resources. A non-coercive pronatalist program would be one that helps women to more easily participate in the labor force and have children, or that provides them with a significant portion of the costs associated with rearing a child (Sobotka et al., 2019). Any program that limits access to existing methods of birth control or penalizes women who choose to be single, childless or have a single child would be a coercive pronatalist policy. States can undertake, and have undertaken, unilateral changes in fertility and abortion policies that suddenly strip women of access to both contraception and abortion, the most notorious example being Romania's 23-year experiment (1967–1990) in seeking to raise its birth rate (Baban, 1999). It was disastrous for both women and children as unwanted children filled orphanages and women experiencing unsafe illegal abortions filled hospital beds. Obviously, low fertility pronatalist countries with high GNIs per capita are in a better position to bear the costs of implementing non-coercive policies. Countries with a history of coercive anti-natalist programs and with governments that believe that it is proper for the state to drive fertility in a desired direction, will be more challenged when it comes to respecting women's reproductive rights, especially if their resources are limited.

The entire low fertility population faces a second significant challenge: fully exploiting the economic growth potential of their demographic dividends. They need to increase savings and invest more in human and physical capital. This will help weather a period of rapid aging and work to ensure a significant second demographic dividend. Having the current active-aged population save to provide for their own later years will lessen the burden faced by the future parental generations, allowing those parents to focus their available resources more on the young than the old. Such a policy, if effective, can act as an indirect pronatalist policy. Every country in this population has already completed its fertility transition. It knows when its transition started and its duration. This gives each country the ability to plot with some degree of precision the size and duration of its first demographic dividend and the general parameters of its potential second demographic dividend (Chap. 6). The challenge is to acquire this knowledge and use it now.

8.7 Conclusion

In 2020 the "developing world" of 1950 is no more. Over the past seventy years the "low," "middle," and "high" fertility groups have experienced very different demographic and development trajectories. All have entered into the fertility transition, but to substantially different degrees. As a result, they face very different fertility and development challenges.

The situation of today's high fertility population of 953 million echoes in some ways that faced by the mid-century developing world: a high TFR of nearly 5 combined with limited development. But the success of their fellow developing countries in traversing the fertility transition means that there are few doubts about their ultimate fate, although many questions about the speed of their progress. The middle fertility population of 702 million has achieved real progress: a TFR decline to 3.3 with significant health and development improvements. It is reasonable to expect that within thirty years this population will largely have joined the low fertility group. The low fertility population of 4.7 billion constitutes the greatest surprise from a mid-twentieth century perspective. The fact that over 70% of the developing world currently has an average TFR of 2.0, significantly better health conditions than were present in the mid-century developed world, and a substantial level of social and economic development is a remarkable, and largely unforeseen, achievement of great importance.

References

Baban, A. (1999). Romania. In H. P. David (Ed.), *From abortion to contraception: A resource to public policies and reproductive behavior in Central and Eastern Europe from 1917 to the present* (pp. 191–221). Greenwood Press.

Barro, R., & Lee, J. (2018). Dataset of educational attainment, June 2018 Revision. http://www.barrolee.com.

Bongaarts, J. (2017). Africa's unique fertility transition. *Population and Development Review, 43*, 39–58.

Caldwell, C., Orubuloye, I. O., & Caldwell, P. (1992). Fertility decline in Africa: A new type of transition? *Population and Development Review, 18*(2), 211–242.

IMF. (2020). World economic outlook database. Washington, DC. Data retrieved July, 15, 2020 from http://www.imf.org/external/pubs/ft/weo/2020/01/weodata/index.aspx.

OECD. (2019). Education at a glance. Paris. Data retrieved July, 15, 2020 from http://www.oecd-ilibrary.org/education/education-at-a-glance-2019_f8d7880d-en.

Scoggins, S., & Bremner, J. (2021). FP2020: The arc of progress 2019–2020, condensed print version. Downloaded March 2022: http://progress.familyplanning2020.org/sites/default/files/FP2020_ProgressReport2020_WEB.pdf.

Sobotka, T., Matysiak, A., & Brzozowska, Z. (2019). Policy responses to low fertility: How effective are they? Working Paper Series, Population and Development Branch, UNFPA. https://www.unfpa.org/publications/policy-responses-low-fertility-how-effective-are-they.

Stover, J., & Sonneveldt, E. (2017). Progress toward the goals of FP2020. *Studies in Family Planning, 48*(1), 83–88.

References

UNDESA. (2019). World population prospects: The 2019 Revision. Rev 1. New York. https://population.un.org/wpp/.

UNESCO Institute for Statistics. (2020). Data centre. Data retrieved July 21, 2020, from http://data.uis.unesco.org.

UNICEF Multiple Indicator Cluster Surveys. (2020). New York. Data retrieved July, 15, 2020 from http://mics.unicef.org/.

United Nations, Population Division. (2022). Estimates and projections of family planning indicators. "Data Portal". Retrieved August 04, 2022, from https://population.un.org/dataportal/home.

United Nations Statistics Division. (2020). National accounts main aggregate database. Data retrieved July, 15, 2020 from http://unstats.un.org/unsd/snaama.

World Bank. (2020). World development indicators database. Washington, DC. Data retrieved July, 21, 2020 from http://data.worldbank.org.

Zeufack, A., et al. (2021) Africa's Pulse, No. 24, October 2021: An analysis of issues shaping Africa's economic future. World Bank. https://openknowledge.worldbank.org/handle/10986/36332.

Open Access This chapter is licensed under the terms of the Creative Commons Attribution 4.0 International License (http://creativecommons.org/licenses/by/4.0/), which permits use, sharing, adaptation, distribution and reproduction in any medium or format, as long as you give appropriate credit to the original author(s) and the source, provide a link to the Creative Commons license and indicate if changes were made.

The images or other third party material in this chapter are included in the chapter's Creative Commons license, unless indicated otherwise in a credit line to the material. If material is not included in the chapter's Creative Commons license and your intended use is not permitted by statutory regulation or exceeds the permitted use, you will need to obtain permission directly from the copyright holder.

Chapter 9
Conclusion

9.1 Introduction

Answers to three important questions emerge from our examination of the developing world's fertility transition. The questions are, first, what have we learned that might be of use to policy makers in contemporary high fertility populations? The UN projects that its 953 million population will be 1.9 billion in 2050 and 3.5 billion in 2100. What actions can help bring about a faster transition to low fertility and slower growth? Second, what are the benefits of declining fertility and slower population growth? Third, what are the global consequences of the 4.7 billion low fertility population's successful completion of its fertility transition? This completed transition has obviously changed the international demographic landscape, but in what ways has it also changed the international economic and policy landscapes?

9.2 What We Know Now that We Didn't Know Back in 1950

Our story started in the 1950s when dramatic mortality decline led to an acceleration of population growth in the developing world. At the time there were many questions about what might happen and what might be done to successfully cope with new demographic challenges. There was very little empirically based knowledge that could be used to formulate successful policies. Today, we have a seven-decade knowledge base from which to offer policy makers in high fertility countries valuable insight into what works.

Several of our conclusions should be useful for policy makers. Fertility levels of developing countries correlate with many socioeconomic variables, including education, child mortality, GDP per capita, and percent urban. Our multivariate fixed effect regression analysis identified girls' education as the most important determinant of fertility. It is about five times more important than child mortality as an explanatory variable for fertility trends. If policy makers wish to hasten their countries' fertility transitions, they should focus resources on schooling, especially schooling for girls. Expending resources on improving child mortality will have an additional fertility decline effect. Since both enhanced schooling and improved child mortality conditions are very desirable ends in themselves, these policy interventions are easy to recommend.

Policy makers should also strive to establish high-quality family planning programs. Our analysis reveals that such a program is likely to produce a rise of 25–35% in contraceptive prevalence and a TFR decline of about 1.5 births per woman. This in turn would lead to a large reduction in future population growth (Chap. 6). Access to a family planning program increases the use of contraception by women who do not want to be pregnant, and thereby reduces unwanted and unplanned fertility. In addition, family planning programs have a substantial impact on the overall demand for contraception, as well as on wanted fertility. Traversing the fertility transition entails women finding themselves with an increasing number of years in which they are fecund and sexually active but want no additional children. Family planning programs will assist women to integrate modern contraceptives into their new fertility regime and allow them to enter the paid labor force. Again, this is a very easy intervention to recommend.

9.3 The Benefits of the Fertility Transition

Once a fertility decline starts the population age structure changes with direct economic benefits. Figure 6.5 showed how substantial the first and second demographic dividends have been during past fertility transitions in the developing world. Between 1955 and 2015 East Asia's GDP per capita (PPP) grew 123% larger than it would have been without the demographic dividends, and South Asian countries experienced more than a 60% larger GDP per capita. In general, developing countries have experienced more rapid rates of economic growth per capita than developed countries. With declining fertility and slowing population growth their GDPs per capita (World Bank, 2022) have been catching up to that experienced by the United States. India's GDP per capita was 5% of that of the US in 1990, and by 2020 it was 10%. Over that period, China's went from 4 to 27%, Chile's from 19 to 40%, Indonesia's from 13 to 19%, South Korea's from 35 to 72%, Vietnam's from 4 to 14%, and Bangladesh's from 4 to 8%. The exception is the high fertility population, where a delayed demographic dividend and more rapid population growth has attenuated economic growth. Sub-Saharan Africa's GDP per capita was 8% of that of the US in 1990 and 6% in 2020.

This economic convergence in living standards is expected to continue in future decades in part due to a substantial second demographic dividend in much of the developing world. For example, the OECD projects that by 2060 India's GDP per capita will be 36% of that of the US, China's will be 51%, Indonesia's will be 44%, and Mexico's will be 39% (Guillemette & Turner, 2018: 16).

In addition to the economic stimulus from demographic dividends, there are several other important benefits from fertility decline: the improvement of maternal and child health, the empowerment of women, the government's increased ability to maintain public capital (e.g., schools, clinics, infrastructure), increased political stability, an improved environment, and a slower depletion of natural resources (Chap. 6). These wide-ranging positive effects of fertility decline should make a government's decision to invest in family planning all the more straightforward.

9.4 The Global Consequences of Low Fertility

The low fertility population's successful completion of the fertility transition has dramatically changed the international demographic landscape. The developed countries (16% of the world's population) already face important demographic challenges: significant population aging, and economic and social problems associated with long-term below replacement fertility. Now an additional 60% of the world's population, the low fertility population in the developing world, finds itself entering into a very similar demographic situation: declining fertility, often well below replacement level, and rapid aging of its population. These trends pose critical population policy challenges which were once limited to the developed world, but have now expanded to encompass over three-quarters of the world's population. This is a very different demographic environment than that existing in 1950.

With the completion of the fertility transition in much of the developing world a new international economic pyramid is emerging, and further significant shifts in countries' economic rankings are likely as the century progresses. According to the OECD (Guillemette & Turner, 2018: 11), the US, Japan, Europe, and 15 other OECD countries produced 52% of the world's GDP in 2020, while India and China produced 34%. As soon as 2040 the OECD's share of the world's GDP is expected to drop to 44%, and India's and China's share to increase to 43%. The world is rapidly becoming a multi-polar one, and this is having a significant effect on how international policy is made. In the first decades after 1950 the overwhelming economic dominance of the West lessened the importance in international affairs of relative human numbers. A country in which a large majority of citizens were impoverished had little political clout even if its population was large. Now, in a world that privileges democratic norms and in which each individual's economic weight is becoming more equal, relative human numbers are assuming a greater political and policy significance.

The fertility transition has produced a new international policy environment, one in which power is more equitably shared, that is indispensable if the global challenges of the twenty-first century are to be successfully met. An enlarged human population consuming natural resources at increasing per capita rates is generating disruptive climate and other environmental changes that recognize no national boundaries. Shortages of vital resources, especially of water, appear likely as this century progresses. Attempts to move populations away from rising coastlines or to resettle those who find themselves living in increasingly inhospitable areas, are much more likely to be successful if jointly made by fully-invested international partners. The fact that an additional 4.7 billion of the world's population has successfully completed its fertility transition has helped create the invested international partners needed to meet these new challenges.

References

Guillemette, Y., & Turner, D. (2018). The long view: Scenarios for the world economy to 2060, OECD Economic Policy Papers 22. OECD Publishing. https://doi.org/10.1787/b4f4e03e-en

World Bank. (2022). World Development Indicators. Retrieved October 5, 2022, from https://data.worldbank.org/indicator/NY.GDP.PCAP.PP.CD.

Open Access This chapter is licensed under the terms of the Creative Commons Attribution 4.0 International License (http://creativecommons.org/licenses/by/4.0/), which permits use, sharing, adaptation, distribution and reproduction in any medium or format, as long as you give appropriate credit to the original author(s) and the source, provide a link to the Creative Commons license and indicate if changes were made.

The images or other third party material in this chapter are included in the chapter's Creative Commons license, unless indicated otherwise in a credit line to the material. If material is not included in the chapter's Creative Commons license and your intended use is not permitted by statutory regulation or exceeds the permitted use, you will need to obtain permission directly from the copyright holder.

The manufacturer's authorised representative in the EU is Springer Nature Customer Service Centre GmbH, Europaplatz 3, 69115 Heidelberg, Germany. If you have any concerns regarding our products, please contact ProductSafety@springernature.com

Printed and bound by CPI Group (UK) Ltd, Croydon, CR0 4YY

25/03/2026

02078233-0002